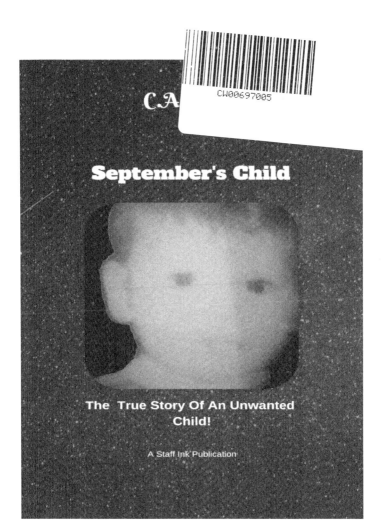

CA

September's Child

The True Story Of An Unwanted Child!

A Staff Ink Publication

TABLE OF CONTENTS

SEPTEMBER'S CHILD

A Remarkably True Story!

C. A. Staff

Copyright © 2013 Carol Staff

DEDICATION

This is for my children - Jess, Wolfgang, Konrad, Katrina, and Amber. You showed me what unconditional love is all about.

To my husband, Trevor, who listens to me, and consistently stands by all I have done, and all I continue to do. Thank You Hunny! You did an awesome job editing my book for me, despite all the drama we went through to get it done. I love you with all my heart! (published)

To my adopted mother, Harriet, for teaching me great strength, teaching me how to read and write, and showing me the only love she could. She was the person who told me I should write a book.

To my adopted dad, Ted, for saving me so many times, for seeing in me what others did not see. "Daddy the morals you have taught me will stay with me long after you are gone."

To my biological mother, Hannah, without her there would be no me.

To all "Adopted Children" everywhere, who have suffered, and or died by the hand of someone who was supposed to have loved them.

To my readers - a special thank you for purchasing, and reading my book. May God Bless You, and guide you through your life.

Thank You Catrina Hernandez from Bridgeport, Nebraska, for your support!

A very special Thank You goes out to my two biggest fans. Tami Yeutter from North Platte, Nebraska, and Sherry Boulton - Wagner from Canada for starting fan pages for me. You two are doing an awesome job!

Facebook Fan Page USA

Facebook Canadian Fan Page

PREFACE

Harriet and Ted Warren were a young happy couple already raising two adopted children. They did everything right. Ted worked hard, bought a home for his small family, and saved up money. Harriet got pregnant. Oh, what a happy day that must have been for the already happy couple.

The Warrens' happiness abruptly came to an end March 1, 1970 with the birth, and death, of their only biological son. One can only imagine how the couple must have felt. To make matters worse the heart broken couple then learned they could not have any more children of their own. They decided on adopting one more baby.

I was born September 22, 1963, to Hannah Polanski. I have found nothing in my files that says Hannah used alcohol while pregnant with me. However by the time I was 6, she was a full-blown alcoholic. Her addiction was the cause of my removal and subsequent adoption. I was the Warrens' third adopted child. They had adopted a son, and then a daughter before me.

I have no recollection of how life was for me before age 4. Some time before that age however, I received four scars on the upper inside right calf of my leg. I was told by my biological mother at our first meeting after I had grown up, that she had cut boils out of my leg with a kitchen knife. At our first adult meeting many years later, that was how she identified me. At that same point in time I was able to meet my biological brothers and sisters.

When my mother lost her parental rights over me, I had one brother, and two sisters. I do not know how she lost my siblings, but she lost them before she lost me. My mother had at some point picked up the pieces of her life, and made a new family with a new husband, thus creating another brother. That is a different part of my story, which takes place in a second book called "Bring On The Rain."

I am a stronger person because of the things I have been subjected to through-out my life. I was in no way a perfect child. At the same time I was not a problem child. I was just a child!

This story is written the way I remember. It is not necessarily the way others remember the same things. I have changed all names in September's Child to protect the dignity of the not so innocent. I have omitted agency names, judges names, and places, including schools as well as teachers, to avoid unnecessary conflict, for those who looked the other way.

This story was not written to point the finger at any one person, place, or thing. It was instead written to show one little girl's will to survive against the odds stacked against her. Being labeled a problem child right from the start set the stage for little Anna to become "The Problem Child."

The pictures in this book are not of me, nor do they have anything to do with me. They are random pictures altered to provide the reader with image impact only. The only photo I have from my past is the one I used for the cover of "September's Child." To my knowledge none of the pictures I have used in the making of this book were copyrighted.

While reading through "September's Child", I hope to show my readers there is a reason for every happening in a person's life. My daddy used to tell me, "What doesn't kill ya can only make ya stronger!" September's Child was written with the hope that the reader can look past the horrible, and unthinkable to see that, "Where there's a will there's a way." (English Proverb)

"September's Child" opens with the memory of waving good-bye to the brother, and two sisters that I did remember having. They were standing in front of a trailer. My brother on the left with a sister next to him, and a smaller sister next to her. I still feel sad thinking about walking away from my siblings.

CHAPTER ONE
WHERE IT
ALL BEGAN

I turned frequently to wave, as mommy ushered me to a waiting car. After mommy put me in the back seat of the waiting car, I got to my knees, and put my hand on the window. Tears rolled down my cheeks as we pulled away from the curb.

After our car ride mommy and I walked towards a building that had a lot of doors and windows. I remember mommy as a pretty woman with long brown hair. She was thin, she had blue eyes, and a smile that always made me smile. I remember feeling sad as we walked on the sidewalk towards the door to our new apartment.

My sadness subsided when I recognized uncle Bud's truck as it pulled up to the curb loaded with our furniture. Uncle Bud brought along another man to help unload the furniture. He took me to a patch of grass, and told me to stay there out of their way. "I don't want to drop something heavy on you, Anna," he warned.

While I sat there picking at blades of grass, uncle Bud and the other man unloaded the truck. I watched as the parade of furniture went past. After the last item disappeared inside the apartment mommy came and held her hand out, which I took. Uncle Bud left with his friend, leaving mommy and I alone to explore our surroundings. I sat at the door as mommy put things away.

Mommy hung a blanket in the doorway where my bed was. The man who had helped uncle Bud earlier came back to see us before I went to bed. He and mommy sat on the couch talking. Mommy told me it was time for bed. She pointed in the direction of the room with the blanket. I laid there and listened to the door open, then shut. Mommy was still there, I heard her humming. It was her humming that sent me off to sleep.

As I started waking up, I looked around my dark room. The blanket, used to keep me from seeing outside my room when I was supposed to be sleeping, was still there. The little room I slept in had walls that were cold to touch. There were no windows in this room.

I was so hungry and weak from lack of food, that it was hard for me to sit up. It was as if something was holding me down. "Mommy", I cried. I laid there waiting. "Mommy", I cried louder. Still no answer. "MOMMY!" I cried as loud as I could. No one came to answer my cries. After I had gone to sleep, mommy had left.

She must have been with that man. Maybe she was sitting outside smoking, or maybe they were talking in mommy's room. I forced my body to move. I wiped my eyes to get the sleep out, and chased my tears away. When I tried to stand it felt as though I had no legs, so I sat back down.

After I moved around a bit, I went to my blanketed door. "Mommy?" I whispered. There was no answer. I went to mommy's open door. I peeked in her room, "Mommy?" There was no one there. I stood at mommy's doorway and looked around wondering what to do. I used the brown couch that sat under the two windows to see outside. Those windows were even with the ground. I saw an occasional car drive by, the grass and the sidewalk. No mommy! I was alone, scared, and hungry.

I slid off the couch, and walked a few steps to the kitchen area. A small round table with two chairs divided the two rooms. I pushed a chair across the floor to look in the fridge. I took the plate of food I saw, put it on the chair and began to eat. As I ate, I heard someone walking around the apartment above me. I heard a door open and shut from above me. I was afraid that someone was coming, but I was hungry, so I continued to eat.

Someone moving the door handle took my attention from the food I was eating. I froze, watching the door. Mommy opened the door! I was happy to see her because I didn't want to be there alone. As fast as I became happy to see her, I remembered that I was eating her food, and she might be mad about that.

She stepped the rest of the way inside. "Anna, what are you doing?" she asked as she tossed her things on the round table. "Hungry", was my reply. She came to me, scooped me off the chair, tossing the food back into the still open fridge. I had made mommy angry, though I didn't understand why. "Hungryyy!" I cried, tears streaming down my face because she had taken away my food. "Oh stop that crying!" she scolded. "Go to bed, you should still be sleeping!" she swatted my behind which sent me back to my little bed. I heard her put the chair back, then I heard her bedroom door shut.

I laid there listening. I wanted to go to her room. I wanted her cuddles. I needed her love. Before I knew it I was sleeping again. The sound of a door shutting hard woke me up again. "Mommyyyy" I cried, I knew she had left, I felt it. I went back out to the living room.

With my little hand pressed against the window, all I could manage was a teary, "Mommyyyyy."

I sat on the couch crying, "Mommy why do you always leave me, I'm hungry mommy." Mommy never ate the food she left in the fridge. I pushed the chair back over, got it out, and finished it. Still hungry, I climbed from the chair to the counter looking for more food. All I found were dishes.

My best friend, and only toy was a worn out teddy bear with one eye. I sat in the middle of the round rug facing the door, holding Teddy tight. Darkness was coming, shadows were forming in our little apartment. I kept glancing at the windows hoping the light would stay.

I thought I saw something run fast across the floor. I held Teddy closer, at the same time drawing my legs up to my chest. I heard noises, but I did not see anything.

I did not like being left alone. I took Teddy to the little round table. Then using a chair I climbed to the table center, and shoved the chairs over. I could hear people walking above me again. I looked in the direction of the windows again, it was dark. I had to stay where I was, until mommy returned. I fell asleep curled up in the middle of the table holding Teddy in my arms.

I woke to mommy asking why I was on the table. I sat up stiff from sleeping there. She paid little attention to me. She seemed more concerned that the chairs needed to be put back. The man who had followed mommy in shifted everyone's attention. He held out a little black puppy, smiling. I looked to mommy for approval. I then looked at the man asking, "Mine?"

He helped me off the table, while mommy tossed Teddy in the trash. I glared at her, retrieved Teddy, saying "NO!" I followed the man to the couch where he put the puppy in my lap. "Shadow", I said. The man seemed happy with the name choice I had made. He smiled, then went with mommy to her room where they closed the door.

Teddy and I were content playing with our new best friend, Shadow. Shadow followed me everywhere. I no longer had to be afraid of the dark, because Shadow protected me. The man came out of the room with mommy a short while later. Mommy said they were going to get some food for Shadow and me. This time it did not bother me that mommy was going. Shadow being there made me feel safe.

Mommy came back with a bag of puppy food for Shadow. She also had a bag filled with crackers, cereal, and other groceries for me. While mommy put everything away, the man took Shadow and me outside to play. Soon it was time to eat, so we all went back in, worn out from playing.

I noticed when we came in that there was a different chair at the table. It was tall, there were three plates on the table with food on them. The man said, "Anna this is a big girl chair for you. Now you won't have to eat on your knees." Being tired and hungry after playing, I ate my food, and climbed off my chair. As I scooped up Shadow and Teddy, mommy told me to get to bed. The muffled voices of mommy and the man sent me off to sleep.

I woke up to Shadow licking my face. I sat up letting him hug me and give me puppy kisses. Then we started the search for mommy. As usual mommy was not there. I got the chair, climbed onto the counter, and picked out two bowls. Lucky Charms was my cereal of choice, it was also the only cereal we had in the freshly stocked cupboards. While filling my bowl I spilled everywhere. It didn't matter, Shadow cleaned it all up.

The more I did for myself, the less I saw of mommy. I was happy to see her when she came home, and sad when she left, but Shadow always made me feel better. Soon it just didn't matter if she was there or not.

Mommy never cleaned me unless we were going somewhere. She barely made sure there was food for me to eat. Once she figured out I could feed myself, she just brought stuff home, made sure I knew where it was, and then left again. I always wore the same clothes, I didn't have many of them. Mommy was usually home to put me to bed. By the time I woke up though, she would be gone.

Sometimes she would bring an uncle home to meet me. She yelled at one uncle because she caught him trying to fondle me through a hole in my dress. Mommy caught him, because I kept saying, "Stop, I don't like that," and struggling about while on his lap. Mommy snatched me off his lap, asked him what he thought he was doing, then screamed, "You get out of my home, and don't you ever come back here." She then slammed the door behind him, putting me down, and telling me to go play. For a long time I thought she was mad at me too.

I can still see the dark smelly places filled with lots of people drinking and smoking, that mommy would often take me to. One time we stayed at one of those places so long that I fell asleep on a bench under a window. Someone covered me with a coat, and piled other coats under my head for a pillow. I received a lot of attention from mommy's friends at those places, but the smells made me feel sick. To this day the bar smell turns my stomach.

It seemed like I had a lot of uncles. I always got bored when visiting my uncles' homes. Whenever I had to leave with mommy, Shadow always welcomed me home. Mommy bought him a red collar and a walking leash so I could take him out to potty. "He's yours, I don't like dogs", she would tell me. "You take care of him."

I did take care of Shadow, and he took care of me. Food was running low again. Shadow had no more dog food, so I shared my food with him. "Come on boy, let's go," I said to him. When I opened the door, out he went, tail wagging, pulling me behind him. While he was doing his sniffing around, a lady came out from the top part of where we lived. She came towards me. She started talking. I knew never to speak with strangers. So when she asked where mommy was, I just pointed and said she was sleeping.

I hurried Shadow back inside, and shut the door, then locked it. Mommy had a run in with the lady when she returned. The lady must have been waiting for her, because she stopped her just outside the door. I heard her say, "Your little girl said you were sleeping."I heard mommy tell her to mind her own business, then she came inside. "Anna, we will be moving again soon." That night as punishment for talking to the lady, I was sent to bed hungry.

Shadow curled up beside me like he always did, and soon we were both sleeping. The next thing I knew, I was waking up to Shadow barking and growling at my feet. I tried to see what was upsetting him, but it was too dark. He jumped off the bed, and was fighting with something. I was frozen with fear. I could hear him cry, then growl, then bark, then yip. I jumped out off the bed and ran to get the broom to help him. He was still whimpering.

In the darkness I saw Shadow laying on the cold floor. With tears streaming down my face, I sat at the edge of my bed calling Shadow's name. I was too young to understand that I had just experienced death. Shadow had fought with, and killed a rat while protecting me.

When mommy got home, I ran to her still scared from what I had witnessed. I took her hand and pulled her to my room, where she saw my Shadow and the rat both dead. She went and got a bag came back put both animals in it and took it to the outside trash. When she came back she said, "These things happen, Anna", then she went to her room. The next day she took me to my aunt's so she could find us a new place.

My aunt's house had a nice wood porch, with three wood steps leading up to it. The floor of the porch was painted a blue-gray color. A white screen door opened to a wood entry door that had four panes of glass in it. Her front room, the color of smashed peas, was where I would sleep on the couch while I stayed there. I stayed with my aunt until mommy found us a new place to live. I overheard mommy telling my aunt that I would be starting school soon, so she would hurry to find us somewhere close to school.

My aunt was a nice happy lady, her home was clean and cheerful. I liked it there, but I missed Shadow, and was having a hard time getting his cries out of my head, especially when it was dark.

After Shadow's death I was convinced that the darkness wanted to take me. At bedtime I would huddle in the corner of my aunt's couch, with my knees tucked up as close to me as I could get them. I would pull the blanket that my aunt had let me use clear up around my neck. Even though aunt Mary and her house were nice, I still did not feel safe there.

I was outside playing with my cousins on the porch when mommy came back. I ran to her, happy to see her. She took my hand, then told my cousins to tell their mom she had taken me. As one of my cousins went in the house, we got into a waiting car, and left.

During the car ride mommy explained that we had a new apartment, and I had a new school. She said, "I can't believe my little girl is going to school already." I had no idea what a school was, but it sounded fun. "What do you do at school?" I asked mommy. "You learn how to read, write, and do numbers there Anna," mommy said. "You will like school, there are other kids your age to play with."

Our new apartment was very much like the last one, except it was not in a basement. It still smelled bad, the white walls looked gray, and the carpet was so stained and dirty you could not tell what its original color was. Being a little girl I was not concerned about where we lived. I just wanted my mommy.

My first day of school was full of fun. We got to color, and we counted. It was just as mommy had said. My time at any school was short-lived. Mommy made me start school five times in one school year. For every new school there was also a new place to live. I don't know what happened to my mommy. She took me to my aunt again, telling her she would be back for me. Mommy never came back for me.

I have no idea how long I stayed with my aunt and uncle. I was chasing my cousins in the alley one day, when I stepped on a piece of glass that went right through my foot. My aunt had to take me to the hospital. While at the hospital my aunt told them that my mommy could not be contacted, because my aunt did not know where she was.

When my aunt received the bill for the care I had received at the hospital, she took it to the Department of Social Services. She just wanted someone other than her to pay my bill. Abandonment charges were filed by Social Services based on what my aunt had told them.

I remember hearing her tell the lady she was speaking with, that I could stay with them as long as I needed to. She just wanted state assistance to keep me with them, until my mommy came back to get me. The state did help my aunt. They paid my bills, and took me away.

CHAPTER TWO THIS IS YOUR LIFE

April 18, 1970, Child Welfare stepped in, mommy was in trouble for abandoning me. A woman from Child Welfare came to my aunt's to get me. "We have to take Anna to a foster home until the Court decides what will happen with her mother." The woman told my aunt.

My aunt said, "We can keep her here with us until her mom is finished with court." My aunt was in tears, and I was clutching her leg afraid of what was going on. The woman told my aunt that I could not stay with family because my mother's parental rights would most likely be taken away from her.

An officer who had been standing by approached me. Seeing him coming towards me, I ran to the house. He caught me at the door, picked me up, and headed to the lady's car. I wasn't going to go without a fight. I kicked and screamed, holding my arms out to my aunt, who was by this time sitting on the porch steps, with her face in her hands, sobbing uncontrollably. "Don't let them take me!" I screamed. There was nothing my aunt could do.

With much struggle, the officer carrying me managed getting me into the lady's car. I tried to open the car door, but could not get it to open. I got on the floor behind the seat, and sat with my back against the door, my knees in my chest, and my chin resting on my knees.

"Anna," the woman from the front seat softly said. "Please get up in the seat, I want to talk to you, but I would like to be able to see you," she said. I reluctantly climbed up on the seat, but I would not look at her.

"Why did you do that?" I asked, still sobbing.

"My mommy is coming back to get me soon," I cried. "Anna your mommy is a very sick woman who won't be able to hurt you any more," she exclaimed. Her statement made me mad. "My mommy has never hurt me!" I screamed at her, "if she's sick she needs me."

The woman kept her calm with me. "Anna, I am taking you to the Wilson's. They are a very nice couple, who have no children, but they like them, and would like to take care of you until we can find you a family." I was afraid of this lady, and afraid of the people I was about to meet. I was afraid of never seeing my mommy again. I was a child I did not understand why this had happened.

We pulled up in front of the Wilson's house. As the car slowed down, the lady looked at me in her rear view mirror. She smiled, put her car in park, and said, "Anna, are you ready to meet the Wilson's?" I just looked away from her. She came around, let me out of her car. she quickly grabbed my hand to keep me from taking off. We headed down the sidewalk to meet Mr. and Mrs. Wilson. "Don't be scared Anna, these people are nice. They will love you," she said.

Mr. and Mrs. Wilson met us at the door. "You must be Anna," she said with a huge smile. "Won't you come in Anna, I would love to show you your new bedroom." She held out her hand, which I took, then she took me to my room. "I guess you have

27

had a rough day, you poor girl. Don't you worry Anna we will take very good care of you here," she said as we walked.

She opened a white door. "Anna this is your room while you are staying with us," she said. "WOW" was all I could say. It was a bright cheery room, with a window for light to come in.

This room would become my safe spot, I thought as we stepped into it. Just as you entered the room was a real bed, with a night stand right next to it. On the night stand was a plastic sheep light, that I could use as a night light. That meant I did not have to be scared that the darkness would come get me like it did Shadow.

There was a window at the foot of my bed with yellow and white flowered curtains you could see through, if you got close enough to the window. Between the window and bed was a tall dresser with clothes in it. I stood for a bit staring at the clothes wondering whose they were.

When Mrs. Wilson figured out what I was looking at, she said, "We knew you were coming so I guessed at your size. I hope they fit you." Across from my dresser was the closet that had a few dresses and shoes in it. I looked around the room. I could be happy here, I thought to myself.

"You want some lemonade, Anna?" Mrs. Wilson

asked me. "Yes," I replied happily. "Follow me, we will go get you some then," she said playfully. Mrs. Wilson was the first person to ever treat me so nice, so she had earned my trust right away.

Mrs. Wilson showed me where to sit when I was eating or drinking, then she handed me my lemonade. She giggled when my face twisted up from the tartness of the lemonade, then she took a drink of hers to show me how it looked. She twisted up her face like I had done, which made me laugh. She smiled at me and said, "See Anna, you and I will get along just fine."

"Tomorrow we will register you for school. Do you like school?" she asked. I told her I did not go to school too much, because mommy was too sick to get up. She said, "That's OK, I will help you every day. You are a smart little girl, before you know it you will catch right up to the other kids."

After we finished up our lemonade, Mrs. Wilson showed me the rest of her house. Where I came through the door earlier was the sitting room, they used that for company. We had just left the kitchen / dining room. There was a family room, that had a television! Oh boy! I had never seen one of those!

Across from my room was Mr. and Mrs. Wilson's room, between was the bathroom. There was a board game room, with a patio door that led to the back yard. The yard had all privacy fencing, and the darkest green grass I had ever seen, and WOW! A swing set!

"It's almost time to have supper, so I tell you what, why don't you watch television until it's time to eat." She pulled a button on the television, which made it come to life. People were talking to each other, I was totally amazed, I looked behind it to see how Mrs. Wilson was making this happen. She giggled at me and said, "You have never seen a television, have you Anna?" I shook my head, no, smiling the biggest smile I ever remember smiling.

She explained to me that the people on the television were actors and actresses. "They act out the shows, while someone uses a TV camera to capture them acting on film. They then take the film to television stations to air them to the public." I listened to Mrs. Wilson wide eyed. This was the most awesome thing ever. She turned the channel to the Munsters, for me to watch while she went to fix supper.

I never laughed so hard in my entire short life. Herman Munster was stamping his feet, saying "No, no, no," then he fell through the floor to Grandpa Munster's lab below. Mr. Wilson came to watch television with me. I smiled, and nodded, when he asked me if I liked this show.

The next show on was The Addams Family, cousin

It was too funny. "Anna, Hunny, wash up, it's time to eat," Mrs. Wilson shouted from the kitchen. "Come on Anna, let's go wash up, I am starving!" Mr. Wilson said.

He took my hand, led me to the bathroom, helped me wash my hands, handed me a towel, then said, "Dry off while I wash my hands." I dried my hands, then handed him the towel so he could dry his hands. "Thank-you Anna!" he said as he dried his hands. "Let's go eat!"

I had never seen so much food, the smells made me realize just how hungry I was. I looked at their smiling faces, and at the many beautiful things. It made me realize I never wanted to go back, nor did I ever want to have to leave here. Mrs. Wilson dished up my plate for me, and said, "When you feel more comfortable here, you can put your own food on your plate. We understand how scary this must be for you."

"Before we eat, we always give thanks for what God has provided us. Anna, fold your hands like this, bow your head like this, and close your eyes. Ready?" Mr. Wilson asked. I quickly nodded a yes. "Lord, let us give thanks for this food we are about to eat, and thank-you, Lord for sharing Anna with us. Amen!" Mrs. Wilson repeated his Amen! I peeked up, to see two smiling faces. "Yes Anna, we can eat now," Mr. Wilson said with a smile.

"Anna, when we finish eating, I will run your bath for you. Do you want help with your bath?" she asked. "Yes," I replied smiling. I ate all the food Mrs. Wilson had put on my plate. Mr. Wilson commented, "I think she liked your food dear." I nodded my approval of his comment. Mrs. Wilson asked if I would like some more. I shook my head, no. Mrs. Wilson got up, came to me, helped me off my chair, then we headed to the bathroom for my bath.

I must have had baths from time to time while with my mommy, or at my aunts house, but they must not have been memorable enough. I do remember getting wiped down plenty of times with a sponge, or wash cloth. I remember mommy used to set me on the counter in the kitchen, and have me put my feet in the sink. She would rub me down with soap, and water, then have me stand to rinse me off.

As Mrs. Wilson was helping me undress, she noticed the dented scars on my leg. "What happened?" she asked. "I don't know, I have always had those," I replied. "Do they hurt?" she asked, gently touching one of my dents. "No, they don't hurt any more." I replied as she helped me into the bath. "You are such a good girl Anna," she was saying as she scrubbed my back. "I just don't understand how anyone could ever hurt you," she said, while scrubbing me clean.

"All done!" she said with a smile. She helped me out of the bath, wrapping a towel around me. "Quickly," she prompted, lets go get your pj's on before you get cold."

I scurried off into my new bedroom, with Mrs. Wilson following closely behind me. She lifted me gently onto the bed, with the towel still wrapped around me. She brought over some pj's that had feet in the bottoms. She pointed out to me that those kind of pj's would help keep my little feet warm.

"The Agency mentioned to me before we got you, that you may have circulation problems, caused by the dents in your leg." She then helped me put my top on, then folded down the sheets and blanket. Then she helped me into bed, tucking the sheets in around me. "You warm enough?" she asked. I nodded a sleepy yes.

Mrs. Wilson stood up to leave the room, then bent down, kissed my forehead, softly saying, "Sweet dreams of rainbows and butterflies, Anna." She turned off my light, and started to shut the door, when she heard me say, "Nooo!" She could see my fear. She asked, "Are you afraid of the dark?" I nodded yes, so she came back to turn on my little sheep light.

"There," Mrs. Wilson's words comforted me as

much as the little sheep light. "You can go to sleep with that on, and I will leave your door open a little. Remember we will be right across from you." I watched Mrs. Wilson leave the room. With a full tummy, and feeling clean, my eyes soon grew too heavy to keep open, and I fell fast asleep.

I woke up feeling happy, and ready for the day. I climbed out of bed. There were no pains, and my legs felt strong, not all wobbly like they used to feel. I crept towards the voices in the kitchen. As I peeked around the corner, Mrs. Wilson greeted me with a smile, a bowl of cereal, and a glass of orange juice. She told me to finish my breakfast so we could get me dressed. She would be taking me to school for registration.

Mr. Wilson finished reading his paper, and got up from the table. He kissed Mrs. Wilson, and kissed my forehead. "See you busy ladies later." he said. "Where is he going?" I asked. "To work," was Mrs. Wilson's reply. I finished my cereal, drank my juice, and scooted off my chair. "Ready," I cheerfully chimed. We headed off to my room to get me dressed. I sat on my bed eagerly watching as Mrs. Wilson carefully chose clothes for me.

Mrs. Wilson chose a pair of little white tights, and a blue and green plaid dress with a white collar for my school registering. On my feet was a pair of shiny black shoes with a strap that went over the top of my foot. She brushed my hair, stood back from me, and told me to turn. I spun a circle, making my dress poof out a little.

Mrs. Wilson, happy with her little creation said, "Such a pretty girl!" That remark filled me with so much happiness, I felt like this lady should have been my real mother. She took me to the car, helped me in, then took her spot behind the wheel, and off we went to go register me.

We pulled up in front of a big brick building. Mrs. Wilson got out of the car and came around to get me. As we walked towards the building I couldn't help feeling a little frightened. She asked me if I was scared. I said, "No, I'm not scared, you are with me." We went inside the building. I looked around as Mrs. Wilson led me to the office.

There were shiny floors, and tall ceilings. Behind us were doors with numbers on them all along either side of the wide hallway. Mrs. Wilson walked me to a door that had "Office" on it. Once in the office she filled out some papers, which did not take long.

The next thing I knew, the office woman was saying, "See you tomorrow, Anna." We were heading back out to the car.

"I don't start today?" I asked Mrs. Wilson. She replied, "No, class has already started, we don't want to interrupt the teacher while she is teaching." On our way home from the school, Mrs. Wilson stopped at a store to get my school supplies for my first day of school. When we got home, we put all my school supplies together in a bag that Mrs. Wilson called a back-pack.

I loved school. There were fourteen children in my class, counting me. My teacher was young, and very nice. She told Mrs. Wilson that I was a fast learner, and was doing great at catching up. I attended school daily. I was happy, and I had made friends at my new school. I had my first ever birthday party, which was also my last ever birthday party.

I celebrated my first memorable Christmas with the Wilsons. I do not remember another memorable Christmas like that. A real Christmas tree was set up in the family game room. The smell of pine, it was so wonderful. Mrs. Wilson baked cookies, and apple pie.
I helped her decorate the house, and the tree. Mr. Wilson had put a Santa with sleigh and reindeer on the roof of their house for me. I thought Mr. Wilson was just coming home from work one day. He came from the roof.

Mr. Wilson excitedly took my hand, and led me outside. "Look!" He pointed upwards, "Santa and his reindeer are on our roof!" I was so excited! The vision in my mind still makes me smile. I experienced more love and care from the Wilson's than I had ever received from anyone in the past six years of my life.

It was the Wilsons who showed me I was worthy of being loved. They treated me like a little girl. We were a family! I lived with the Wilsons, where I was treated like their daughter, for the duration of my mommy's court sessions, which I never heard about.

While I was getting comfortable with the Wilson's however, Social Service workers, and Adoption Agency workers were busy finalizing my adoption to a family who really did not want me. The Warrens wanted a baby, they did not want a child who was almost seven years old.

While speaking with a psychologist at one point in my life, I was informed that instead of settling for me the Warrens should have searched for and adopted a new born baby. Even if that meant going through a different agency. It seemed that Harriet's loss had not been dealt with properly.

She never was able to bond with the son she had lost.

My psychologist explained to me that had the Warrens adopted a baby at birth, and had that baby been a boy, Harriet would have been able to heal. I think that Harriet did not see her own problems though, and I became her problem. There was nothing I could do, nothing I could change. I was a child, who had to accept what was given. Back then children did not have voices. They were to be seen, not heard.

The Wilsons wanted me. They had asked the agency if they could adopt me. They were denied, because they were foster parents, and they lived in Omaha. The Wilsons living in Omaha meant that if my biological mother ever did try to find me, it would have made it easier for her to steal me because I was there.

I often wonder how different my life would have been, had I been allowed to stay with the Wilson's.

CHAPTER THREE
UNWANTED
PATH

Decem ber 22, 1970, my biological mother's parental rights were ended by the court. The court then asked Adoption Services to find me an adoptive home. I had no idea that while I was celebrating my first real Christmas, the wheels of fate were turning in a direction that would eventually nearly break my spirit. I was clueless that the New Year was going to end up bringing me more pain than I had ever felt.

The cold winds of January were bringing me Harriet Warren. Yes, it was all being set up. My future was in the hands of a person sitting at a desk arranging my adoption with a well-educated woman, who had nice phone manners, and was a woman of the church. Harriet Warren was a city girl from Iowa. She had been raised by strict parents. She was very good at hiding her true self from the outside world. She hid herself behind her husband. Ted Warren was Nebraska raised, had joined the Army, and was a God fearing man, who came from a large, respectable pioneer family. Ted Warren loved his wife so dearly, that he would have done anything to protect her. The couple had already adopted two other children as babies.

"Anna," Mrs. Wilson called to me. "You have a meeting today with a family who may want to adopt you." My heart sank! Mrs. Wilson came to sit by me, she noticed the change in my facial expression. I did not want to meet anyone else. I was happy being here. She put her arm around me, and snuggled me. She said, "You trusted me, Anna, it's time for you to learn you can trust others as well." I could not go to school that day, an Agency woman would be picking me up soon. A dark blue car pulled up in front of the house. "I think she's here," I said. It was cold outside.

Mrs. Wilson bundled me up in my coat, pulled my mittens on my hands and pulled my sleeves over my mitten tops. Then she pulled my hood over my hair, tucking my hair into the hood, and secured the hood by tying it under my chin.

The Agency woman was almost to the door. Mrs.

Wilson opened the door, patted my behind, and said, "Anna, remember what I said, you have to learn to trust others." I smiled at her, hoping I would be coming back to her after this meeting. The woman rushed me to her car, it was so cold outside, I was glad to be in her already warm car.

We arrived at the Agency, another big brick building, that had glass front doors. The lady that had driven me there rushed me inside to the warmth. She handed me over to another Agency lady, whose name was Sharon. Sharon rushed me down a hall taking my coat and mittens, and straightening my hair as we went.

Sharon opened the door to a small room. "Anna," she said, "can you be a good girl, and wait in here until I get back?" I nodded, and looked around the room.

There was a chair by the door we had come through, so I went over and sat in it and waited. As I sat, I took in my surroundings. There was a long, skinny mirror on the wall in front of me. A small table with two chairs positioned opposite each other was to my left. In the corner was a toy box filled with baby toys. To my right was a baby crib. I thought to myself, "I'm not a baby." I wandered over to the toy box, rummaged through it a bit, found it was actually all baby toys, so I returned to my seat by the door.

"She's just sitting there," Harriet said, from the other side of the mirror. "She doesn't seem to be a very happy child," Ted replied. "Anna is what we call a problem child," Sharon explained. She handed the couple Anna's agency file, and continued. "Anna has endured extensive neglect, as well as physical abuse, as you can see from her file. Children like Anna do well with structured homes, and respond best to strict discipline."

"We realize you were looking forward to adopting a baby. However, you have adopted two babies already, it is clearly stated in our agencies policy, that once you have adopted two Caucasian babies, you must adopt an ethnic baby, or an older child like Anna."

Because this adoption agency only allowed two babies to be adopted to one family, the Warrens should have chosen to adopt from a different agency, instead of settling for me. "When you are ready I will take you to meet Anna, and if you are still unsure, I will bring you baby Angelina. Angelina is an African-American baby girl."

The sound of the door opening startled me. "I told you I would be back, Anna, and look I have brought some nice people to meet you." Sharon explained to me.

I stood up because that is what you were supposed to do when you met new people. She continued to introduce the strangers to me, "This is Ted, and this is Harriet, they may want to adopt you, Anna. I will leave you three alone now to get acquainted. When you are ready, Ted, I will bring baby Angelina into to meet you as well."

I looked at Harriet. She was short with dark brown curly hair, and green eyes. Then I looked at Ted. He had brown hair, and blue eyes like mine. He was a tall and strong looking man. I just stood there smiling at them.

Ted asked, "Should we go over here, and color a picture?" I said, "Ok." He gently put my little hand in his, and we walked over to the table. "Harriet," he said, "why don't you come join us?" He got up and went to get the chair by the door for his wife, at which point they both joined me at the table.

The thing I noticed the most about Ted was his hands. His hands were huge, and they looked strong. He was very gentle with his hands though. Ted did most of the talking, asking me what color to make the tree, grass, and the sun in the picture we were coloring.I think he was testing me.

Harriet asked me my name, and how old I was. Other than that, she didn't say much. I felt like she was inspecting me, trying to decide if I was worthy of their adoption or not.

It seemed like only a few minutes had passed before Sharon entered the room again. She was carrying a baby, which she handed to Harriet. "It was nice to meet you, Anna," Ted said.

I smiled, and returned his departing words, "It was nice meeting you too." Harriet said, "We will see you again soon, ok?" I said, "Ok." I gave her a quick hug, and a smile, which she returned with an awkward hug and pat.

I think I surprised her. Sharon then whisked me out the door to a lady in a car that was waiting for me outside the building. Sharon said, "This lady will take you back to your foster home." I nodded as I climbed in the back seat of the car. When the door was closed, we pulled away from the curb in the direction of my foster home.

"How did you like the Warrens?" the lady driving asked me. "The what?" I asked. "The people you just met, did you like them?" I replied, "Oh yes, I liked them. They were nice." Before I knew it we were parking in front of the Wilson's house. I got out and ran to the door.

Mrs. Wilson greeted me with a big hug and kiss on the forehead before I headed off to the safety of my room. I sat on the edge of my bed, and thought, this was my home. I definitely didn't want to ever leave. Maybe those people I just met won't like me, then I could just stay here.

Mrs. Wilson came to talk to me about the meeting I had. She asked me how I thought things went. I told her I didn't think the lady liked me, but the man was very nice, and had big hands. "Would you like to go live with them?" Mrs. Wilson asked me.

I said, "NO! I like it here, why do I have to leave? Did I do something wrong?" She looked at me with sad eyes, and took my hands in hers, and told me that there were rules against foster parents adopting the children they took care of. "But if I could, I would make you my daughter," she added.

As I got more and more comfortable at the Wilson's home, the Adoption Agency was getting all their necessary paperwork finished up. Even though I was not the baby Mrs. Warren had wanted they had agreed to adopt me. Not a single day has gone by that I have not wished at some point that the Warrens had not wanted to adopt me. For the sake of Harriet Warren, and myself, I wished that they had been able to find their baby.

Mrs. Wilson was getting me ready for school. We had to get all my Valentine's cards for my classmates put together. She packed my lunch in a brown paper bag. "Anna, hurry or we will be late for school," she said. She was standing at the door patiently waiting for me. As I came running past her she handed me my brown paper bag lunch.

I ran out the front door, and waited for her at the car. She shut the door to the house, and came to help me get into the car. "Off we go," she said. Within a few minutes she was dropping me off at my school.

At the school Mrs. Wilson kissed my forehead, before I left the car. I was happy because it was almost Valentine's day. I was even happier because it had been a long time since my meeting with those people, so I thought that they must not have wanted me.
They must have decided on adopting the baby. I was so wrong....

My class was excited about our Valentine's celebration. We had made our hearts the day before. Our hearts were two pieces of colored paper cut into the shape of hearts, and then sewn together with different colors of yarn. After recess was when we got to have our celebration. It was so much fun handing each classmate a card. We played games, ate heart-shaped candies, and listened to our teacher tell us about Valentine's day.

It was getting close to time for school to be over, so the teacher told us to put our cards in our heart-shaped envelopes. The lady from the office came in to speak to the teacher, who looked at me, then said, "Alright."

"Class, I have an announcement," our teacher said, as she looked at me. "This is Anna's last day here, so we all need to wish her the best as she goes to her new home." I was confused! The bell rang for school to be over, we all stood up to line up at the door, everyone passed by me giving me a hug, and telling me they would miss me.

One little girl asked if she would ever see me again. The teacher replied, "Maybe," to her. Mrs. Wilson was at the door waiting for me. I ran to her. "Is it true?" I asked. "Yes, it is," she replied. I walked to the car with Mrs. Wilson, head down, and tears streaming down my cheeks. I was sad beyond belief. The next few days we were busy getting my things packed up.

February 18, 1971, I was ready, but I was not willing to go. Mrs. Becker, another Adoption Agency lady, came to get me. We put my two little bags by the door, and waited for her arrival. I sat on the couch in the sitting room, head down, tears dripping on my leg.

The Wilsons had taught me to pray before eating meals, pray before bed, and pray if you were
searching for an answer. They had taught me to
believe in the power of prayer.

I was deep in silent talk with God when Mrs. Wilson came to sit with me. She looked as sad as I
felt. She put her arm around me, and said, "I'm not
going to ask you if you're ready, because I know
you don't want to go, but sometimes what we
don't want, is what's best for us.

You are a very loveable little girl Anna, your new
family is lucky to be getting you, they will love
you just like we do." A gray car pulled up outside.
I tried to make a run for my room, but Mrs. Wilson
caught me.
Mrs. Wilson consoled me until she managed to
calm me down enough to talk to me. She handed
me some pictures. "Anna, keep these pictures always. These are your sisters, and brother, and this
one is you." She said while pointing to the people
in the pictures. "Your Aunt asked me to hold those
for you, until it was time to give them to you."

I tucked the pictures into my heart-shape Valentine's bag, and held on tight to it. Mrs. Wilson took
me to the car, and gently lowered me into the seat.
"Anna, I truly enjoyed you being here with us.

Now you be a good girl for your new family." As the car moved away, Mrs. Wilson stood her ground, waving until I could no longer see her. That was the last time I ever saw Mrs. Wilson, or my classmates, or my teacher. However, I have never forgotten the kindness I received from them.

CHAPTER FOUR
PROBLEM CHILD

T he Warrens were waiting for me at the adoption agency. Mrs. Becker pulled up behind their car. She looked back at me and asked, "Are you ready, Anna?" I felt far from ready, but I knew I didn't have any other choice, so I said, "Yes." Ted unloaded my two little bags out of the car, while Harriet came to get me.

Harriet opened my door, and said, "Hi Anna, I told you we would see you again soon." She smiled at me. Even though she was smiling at me, I still felt so scared and uneasy. "Why does this lady scare me so much?" I thought to myself. "Come on," she smiled again, and offered her hand to me. Harriet tried to get me to give her my heart envelope, but I refused to give it up, so she took my hand and walked me to their car.

Harriet opened the car door, and said "Anna, this is your new younger brother Andy, and the little girl next to him is your new little sister, Crystal."

I gave an uneasy smile, and said "Hi." Then I got into the car. I looked out the window and watched my new parents talking to Mrs. Becker.

They turned, and headed towards the car. Ted climbed into the driver's side seat, and Harriet got in the passenger side. "Where to?" he asked Harriet. She said, "Let's go to Burger King for some lunch, before we get on the road to go home." He gave a light chuckle and said, "Your wish is my command."

Eating at Burger King was the first I had experienced fast food. I had a burger and fries. It was sooooo good, to this day Burger King is my favorite fast food restaurant. After filling our tummies, it was time to use the rest room, so we could get on the road. Harriet took Crystal and me, and Ted took Andy. We all met at the doors leaving Burger King to walk to the car together. It felt pretty good walking with a family, but I just did not feel like I fit in with these people.

Though I was with four other people, I felt all alone. Ted drove wherever Harriet said she wanted to go. We went shopping at K Mart, a yarn place, and other places. The last few places she went into by herself, while we all sat waiting for her. We were all getting tired, Crystal fell asleep, Andy was close to falling asleep, I was yawning, Ted was reading something. Ted glanced at us, and asked, "You kids tired?" Andy and I said, "Yes, a little".

When Harriet got back to the car, she noticed Crystal had fallen asleep. She suggested to Ted that they get a motel room for the night, and go home tomorrow. Ted started the car, then began his search for a motel. I had never been to a motel, but I just could not gather the courage to ask what a motel was. I was still very uncomfortable with my new family.

After a lot of driving, Ted said happily, "There it is, a Days Inn." He pulled right up to the doors of the building, and got out of the car. He went inside, stood at the counter talking to a man, who gave him something, then he came back to the car, smiling.

"Our room is right around here," he said. He drove around the corner of the building, then started looking for something. "There it is, room 26". He pulled up to a door that had a 26 on it. Harriet and Andy started getting out of the car. Ted said "I will get our little sleeping girl." Harriet said, "Come on Anna, you can come with me."

I followed Harriet through the door into a room that had two big beds with a table between them, with a light on the table. There was a long dresser on the right side, with a TV on top of it. I heard Andy tell his mom, "She's stupid, she doesn't even know what to do." Harriet gave a little giggle, then noticing my reaction to his comment, she said, "That's not very nice Andy! Now you go get your jammys on, then go sit on the bed." That's all he got for saying what he did.

Ted came back in with my suit case and a bunch of other stuff. I went to him to get my suit case. I said, "Thank you," and smiled, though inside I felt like crying. I wished for Mrs. Wilson, and my safe room at her house.

Harriet told me to get my jammys on and get in the bed. I did as I was told. Crystal was already sleeping in the middle of one of the beds, so after I got my jammys on I climbed in next to her.

Andy came over and said, "That's my spot!" so I got up, and went to the other side, near the window. Andy got in bed content that he got what he wanted. I laid on my back, closed my eyes, and wished I could be anywhere but there. Harriet turned out the light between the beds. The only light in the room, was from a street light shining in the window.

I had a fingernail biting habit. When I got nervous I would chew on my nails. I had something stuck in my bottom front tooth that was bothering me, so I tried to pick it out. I held my hand up to the light from the window to see if I had gotten it. The next thing I knew Harriet was there yelling at me.

Harriet slapped me across the face. Everyone in the room must have heard it. She grabbed a handful of my hair, and pulled me out of the bed. She took me to my suitcase still holding my hair. By this time I was crying. I had no idea what I had done to deserve this treatment. Until that point I had no memories of anyone ever hitting me.

Harriet let go of my hair, got a pair of socks out of my suitcase, and put them on my hands. "KEEP THOSE ON YOUR HANDS!" she yelled. "They told me you had a nail-biting habit, and that you were going to be a problem child. Get back in bed, and go to sleep."

Harriet's next slap knocked me off my feet. I scooted out of her reach, got up, and ran to the bed. I got in bed and pulled the blanket up around my neck. I wanted to tell her to take me back. I wanted to go back to my home. I even thought about my mommy. I could not remember ever being hit like that.

I laid there trying to stifle my sobs, so she would

not know I was still awake. I heard Ted tell Harriet that she had been too hard on me. I heard Harriet say, "She has to learn." My last thought before I quietly sobbed myself to sleep was, "I hate you".

When I woke up, the first thing I did was check to see if the socks were still on my hands.One had fallen off, so I hurried to feel for it. I had to get that back on, before she saw it was off. I found the sock, put it back on, then gingerly looked to the other bed to see if anyone else was awake.

Harriet was sitting up on the edge of the bed, facing away from me. So I rolled back over as quietly as I could. I could hear everyone starting to get up. Ted and Harriet were in the bathroom area, getting dressed and ready for the day. Crystal and Andy were sitting on the bed, but I was too afraid to move.

I heard Harriet say to Ted, "I guess I better get the kids ready to go." I sat up on the edge of the bed to wait for her commands. Harriet was helping Crystal get dressed. She said, "Andy, Anna, get dressed, put your jammys in your suitcase, then take them to your dad, he is loading the car, and hurry." I was hoping that after what happened the night before, they were taking me back to the agency, so I could go home.

Harriet was making sure everything was out of the room. Ted was waiting for his wife with us kids in the car. I cautiously asked him if I could go home now. His answer was, "We are going home as soon as your mom gets to the car." I felt like saying, she isn't my mom, and I don't want her to be my mom, but I just sat back in my seat, because she was coming to the car.

I turned my head and looked out the window, to avoid looking at Harriet at all. When she spoke to me I responded politely, after that I made sure to look away from her. I didn't want to do anything to make her angry with me.

I liked sitting by the window, I could see everything we passed, even though there wasn't much to see. My heart envelope was laying on the floor of the car, untouched, so I reached down to pick it up. My movement in the back seat must have alerted Harriet, she looked back at me. "What are you doing Anna?" she asked. I held up my envelope, and replied, "Just getting this." She asked, "What do you have in that?" I replied, "Just cards from school." Harriet said, "Let me see it please."

I didn't want her to see it, my pictures were in there. "Let me see it, Anna," she repeated, annoyed that I had not just handed it to her. I just knew if I made her mad she was going to reach back there to slap me like she did the night before, so I reluctantly handed her my heart full of treasures. She snatched it out of my hands, and started going through it.

My heart sank when she found the pictures! "Who are the people in these pictures, Anna?" she asked. "The one picture is me, and the other one is me with my brother, and sisters." I replied. "My sisters, brother, and I," she said was the proper way to say what I had said to her. I nodded, then looked down, to avoid her glaring at me.

I knew I had said something wrong. I was powerless against this lady. Harriet kept my treasures, from that day on. I never saw them again. I leaned back in the seat, a tear streamed down my cheek, I thought to myself, don't let her see you cry, that will make her mad, so I turned my head to watch out the window again. Eventually I drifted off to sleep, my dreams lumbered with ways to get away from Harriet.

The car slowing down woke me up. I sat up a bit in my seat wiped my eyes, and tried to make out where we were. Ted was pulling up next to another car.

"Ok kids, let's all go use the bathroom." Harriet said. "It's going to be a while before we get home," she said. We got out of the car, and I followed Harriet to a building, where we went in. "This way." she said. I followed. "Go in one of those stalls, and use the potty," she said. "We still have a while before we get home, and daddy doesn't want to make any more stops."

I did as I was told. We finished up, washed our hands, and left the little building to go back out to the car. Ted and Andy were already outside the building. Andy was running around, and Ted was at the car, moving things around. Harriet had Crystal, so I just followed her. We all took our spot back inside the car. Ted backed the car out of where we were, and off we went. Harriet handed us all some grapes. I said, "Thank you," sat back, and picked at my grapes.

Ted and Harriet were chatting in the front seat, I was watching the world go by out my window, and Crystal and Andy were playing with the toys they had brought with them. I heard Ted say, "Oh my, I didn't realize we were so close to our turn off." I wondered if we were close to getting to their house, so I started paying attention to what was going on out my window.

Ted was getting off the interstate, then he turned left at a stop sign. Up and over a bridge that crossed the interstate. Down the road a-ways Ted turned right, and we passed a school. Harriet said, "Anna that is where you will be going to school." I smiled. Down the road a bit further, Ted turned left, he glanced to the back seat, Andy was getting excited, I thought we are almost to their home.

The road we were on had houses on both sides of it. At the end there was a big house on a hill, part of the road went left, the other part went right. Ted took the left part, followed it around a bend, went a little bit further, then turned left. "Here we are" he said. Their driveway went all the way around their house.

Ted said, "Hold on!" Up the driveway he went, around the right side of the house coming to a stop behind their house. "Anna, this is your new home." he said. Harriet said, "Yes! Welcome home," she smiled. Andy opened the car door, and got out, Harriet got out and came to the back door to get Crystal. She said, "It's ok Anna, you can get out now." I smiled and got out of the car.

To me, that was the most beautiful house I had ever seen. (However it soon became the worse house ever.) It was even nicer than the Wilson's house. It was big, and red brick, and it had glass doors that everyone was going into. There was a swing set with a slide too. Ted had gone into a different door than we were going into, but he had opened the glass doors from the inside of the house.

Harriet put Crystal down inside the house, then she came back to me. "Come with me Anna, I will show you your new home." I thought maybe she isn't so mean after all, she was just away from home, she's happy now. She took my hand, and led me around the house. Inside the glass doors, there was a big, nice table with a nice hanging light above it. "This is where we eat," she said. "Over here is the kitchen," she pointed to the right. Harriet led me to the living room. "This is where we sit together after we eat," she said. She then led me down a short hallway. "This is Andy's room, this is the bathroom, this is daddy's and I room, and this is your room that you will share with Crystal."

Harriet led me into my new room, where there was a big bed. There were two windows, one above the bed, the other on the right side of the room, a big dresser, and an even bigger closet. She let go of my hand. "Take your clothes out of your suitcase, and put them in your side of the dresser."

"This is your side of the dresser," Harriet showed me which side I could have. She pulled each drawer out to show me where to put my clothes. Top drawer, socks, and panties. Next drawer down shirts, with the last drawer for pants. She said, "Now you put your things away while I go help daddy." I said, "Ok." As I watched her leave the room, I thought she looks happy now, maybe I will like it here.

My suitcase was on the bed, so I pulled it to the edge, opened it, and began to put my things away, just exactly how Harriet had told me to. I was so happy with myself. I ran out of the room to go tell Harriet I had finished what she had told me to do. "I put my things away", I said happily. "Let's go see how you did", Harriet said.

I followed Harriet back to the bedroom.

Harriet pulled the top drawer open, and said "Oh no, this just will not do, Anna! You just dumped everything in here, you have to match up your socks, then fold them like this." She took a pair of socks out of the drawer and folded one sock over the other sock. "You try now," she said. I did as she had done, it wasn't as nice as what she had done, but she seemed happy with it, because she smiled down at me. "Very good Anna," she said. She then showed me how to fold my panties.

Harriet told me to fold everything in that drawer, then come get her so she could show me the next drawer folding. She left me to finish my task. I was eager to learn, and even more eager to please Harriet. Because she had told me I was going to be a problem child, I felt I had to prove to her I would not be.

As I finished putting away my last pair of socks, folded just the way Harriet had told me to. I tried to think of ways I could make Harriet happy. I came up with an "Ah-ha!" moment. I took a shirt out of the next drawer, and a pair of my pants out the other drawer, then took them to Harriet who was by this time sitting in the living room knitting. "Did you finish your folding?" she asked as I approached her sheepishly. "Yes," I replied, "will you show me how to do these, please?"

I held out my shirt, and pair of pants for her to see. My "Ah-ha!" moment saved her from having to come to me, and interrupt what she was doing. She seemed pleased, she smiled at me, and said, "Just let me finish this row." I watched her intently, pleased with myself for being able to make her smile. She finished her row, carefully put it aside, and reached out for my shirt.

I handed it to her, ready to watch. "This is how you fold a shirt, Anna." she said. She laid it out in front of her, folded one side in to the middle, then the other side in to meet up with the first side, then she folded it in half. "See," she said, "nice and neat." She then took the pants I was holding, and held them up. She said, "See these bumps here," she held them close so I could see what she was talking about. I nodded as she looked at me to see that I was understanding what she was talking about.

Harriet then continued, "Those are seams. You match up the seams like this, that makes it have a nice folded line," she showed me the line on the pants she was wearing. "You see?" I said, "Yes, I see." After she matched up the seams, she folded the pants over, then over again. I said, "Thank you," smiled at her, then went to finish my other two drawers. I put the already folded shirt and pants on the bed, so I could refer to them while folding the others that were in my drawer.

As I carefully folded each shirt, then each pair of pants, I thought this is not so bad. I could not help but smile to myself. It seemed to me the night before was just a one time event. I really wanted to believe that, I really wanted a mother, and Harriet was a nice mother to have when she smiled at me.

I finished up my clothes, placing every item in nice neat rows in my drawers, then I carefully closed each drawer, so I would not mess up my good work. I wanted more smiles from Harriet, I needed more approval. As I left the room I almost ran into Harriet coming to check my progress. Perfect I thought.

Harriet asked me if I had finished my folding. "Yes," I said proudly. "Well let's see how you did this time," she said. Harriet opened each drawer, inspecting closely. She said "Very good Anna, you do learn quickly." She was happy with me, she put her hand out to me, and said, "Come with me, you can help me fix supper." I was ecstatic to be able to please Harriet, this meant she would accept me.

Harriet was a very pretty lady when she smiled and laughed. She handed me the plates, snapping me back to reality. I followed her to the table where she explained to me that for every chair there needed to be a plate in front of it. "Don't put the plates too close to the tables edge," she said. "Someone might tip a plate of hot food into their lap if it was to close to the edge."

Harriet showed me how to set the silverware next. Big fork on the right side of the plate, little salad fork next to the big fork. The butter knife was to go on the left side of the plate, with the spoon on the outside of it. Glasses for beverages were to go at the top right corner of each plate.

While we were setting the table, Harriet noticed my flaw. I was left handed. Harriet asked me what hand I used the most. I said, "This one," and held up my left hand smiling, not realizing that was the wrong answer.

Harriet said, "Anna, go get everyone, it's time for supper." I started to yell, "Everyone.." but was stopped by a firm hand on the back of my neck, sharp finger nails digging in enough to hurt. "I said, go tell them, not yell!" she said sternly. "Ok," I whimpered. As I headed down the short hall to Andy's room, I wondered what I had done this time to make her hurt my neck.

I peeked into Andy's room, saw him playing with his cars on a round rug beside his bed. "Time to eat," I said then went to get Crystal. After getting her, I went to the couch to get Ted. "I heard," he mumbled, "let's go eat."

With everyone sat down in their chairs at the table, the evening prayer was said. "Dear God, thank you for this food we are about to receive, and Lord, thank you for the newest member of our family, Anna, and Lord guide us through our lives, so we may prosper through the gifts you provide us. Amen."

There was light discussion while we ate our supper, with Ted asking Harriet how she was doing with me, and Harriet telling him how well I had done until she had told me to get everyone for supper. I had annoyed her, with my antics she was saying. I just quietly ate my food, not wanting to annoy her any further. After supper it was time to learn how to clear the table, and do the dishes. Since Harriet was helping me, Ted took care of helping Andy and Crystal take their baths, and get ready for bed.

Harriet filled up one sink with soapy water, the other with just water. "Since it is late, and I want to get these dishes done, I will show you how to do the dishes, you will pay attention," she said. "Tomorrow you will do the dishes, and I will dry them." She handed me a towel. "You dry, Anna!" she ordered. We did the dishes together, then while I was finishing up drying them, Harriet left to go fill the tub for my bath.

I didn't need help like the other kids, because I was older, so she left me to take my bath. When she came back she had a towel with her. She said "Are you finished, Anna?" I said "Yes." I started to get up, then she noticed my hair was not wet. "Oh no you don't," she scolded, "you have not washed your hair, what have you been doing in here?" she asked. She put hair soap in her hand, then put it in my hair.

Harriet scrubbed my head so hard with her finger nails I thought my head must been bleeding. After she rinsed the soap out of my hair, she put the towel on the floor. "Get out, dry off, get your jammies on then go to bed."

I did exactly as I was told. Crystal was already asleep by the time I got there, so I got into bed very quietly. Harriet came to the door to make sure I was in bed, I acted like I was sleeping, so she left. Tears streamed down my cheeks, softly landing in my pillow, as I cried myself to sleep my first night at my new home.

CHAPTER FIVE
ROCKY ROAD

T ed had gone to work before all the rest of us were up the next morning. Crystal woke me up getting out of bed. I heard her feet thump as they hit the floor. Then I listened as she ran into her mommies room. I could hear Harriet playing with her daughter, Crystal laughing, followed by Harriet laughing, soon I heard Andy run into the Warren's room. I did not dare go in that room. I did not fit in there.

"Anna, time to get up," was the next thing I heard. She came in with Crystal, to get her dressed. I was already sitting on the edge of the bed. She got a pair of pants out of my drawer for me, and a shirt out of my other drawer, then told me to get my socks myself. As I quickly got dressed, she dressed

Crystal. She told me to fold my jammies and put them under my pillow.

Then Harriet said, "Pull the sheets up on the bed on both sides, then pull the blanket up the same way. Fold the blanket back, place the pillows at the fold, and put the blanket over the pillows." That was how she expected me to do the bed every morning except Sunday mornings, which I learned was bedding wash day.

Harriet was nothing like Mrs. Wilson. She was grumpy almost all the time, when she wasn't grumpy she was annoyed. She always assumed that I should know whatever she was trying to teach me, then would be angry with me for asking her how to do whatever it was she was wanting me to do. It seemed like every time I walked into the room Harriet's face would turn into a scowl. I could not understand why she hated me so much. I could understand even less why she had adopted me.

The Warrens were told by the adoption agency that I would have to have an eye exam, and a physical within two weeks after they took me home. The eye doctor, and the doctor doing the physical would have to fill out the paperwork Harriet gave to them, and return it in the mail to the agency themselves. All Harriet had to do was set up the appointments, and take me there.

I passed the physical which made Harriet pretty happy, however my eyes were very bad. I needed glasses. The eye doctor dilated my eyes, which made my eyes hurt when I opened them. He also gave me a patch to wear over my good eye because I apparently had a lazy eye. My left eye did not like doing it's share of work he explained to me, Harriet waited for me in the waiting room.

The Eye Dr. explained to me that I would have to have glasses. The glasses would have a very strong prescription that my eyes would not be used to. I would be able to see things much clearer, but the glasses might give me headaches for a while. He also told me that if I did not wear my glasses every day, I would be blind in less than 5 years.

I used the eye patch all day, every day for two weeks. Harriet made me take naps every day for exactly one hour. This was supposed to allow both eyes the rest they needed from the work they were not accustomed to. When my glasses came in my eyes were ready for them. Since the eye doctor had warned me about going blind if I did not wear my glasses, I wore my glasses everyday without fail.

We had bowls of cereal for breakfast. I washed and dried the bowls after we finished. This was a daily occurrence, with the exception of Saturdays, as well as Sundays. Saturdays, and Sundays were pancake days. Ted would make pancakes in the shapes of animals, and Mickey Mouse.

Crystal and Andy always went to play after breakfast. When it was too cold to play outside they played in Andy's room. Right away Harriet showed me how to vacuum, which became my chore. It did not take me long to figure out the reason Harriet wanted to adopt me. She wanted me because I was old enough to be her housekeeper.

Every day she taught me more. After my first week with my new family I was taught how to dust, wipe plants, wash windows, vacuum, and start laundry. I also started school. School was never first. First came chores, school came in between. I'm sure she made it this way so I would hurry through my chores, because I loved doing school work.

I could see no difference between Crystal, Andy, and myself, except that they were there before me. Andy was only two years younger than me, yet all he ever did was complain about me, and play. Crystal was two years younger than Andy.

Crystal was way too young to be subjected to the things I was subjected to. My new home soon became just that, a home. My new family was a family minus me. There was no love for me, every thing I received there I had to earn, by jumping

Harriet's hurdles. Harriet made it look as though I was loved, as long as we were in public, or around her friends.

I was so far behind my classmates, because I had never really gone to school when I should have, with the exception of the part year I went while living at the Wilson's. It was evident I would have to take kindergarten over. That was strike one against me. Strike two was I had a speech problem. I was having problems pronouncing S's. Strike three was that I was left handed. For strike two there would be therapy at school in the mornings twice a week for several months, that would fix my speech problems.

Strike three Harriet herself would fix by tying my left hand behind my back, and making me use my right hand. For the longest time I could use both hands equally as well. No matter what I did to try to make Harriet happy with me, there was always going to be something about me she did not like.

Let's go back to correcting my speech. Every school day started the same. I would go to class, role call was first, followed by the pledge of allegiance, after which homework was handed in. There would be a knock on the door, where my speech therapist would remove me from class. I would spend the rest of the morning reciting : Sammy was a garner snake, his skin was shiny green, all day he made a hissing sound, and tried not to be seen. Sssssssss. There was also "Sally sold sea shells down by the sea shore."

I recited those lines so much they were permanently etched into my memory. In the beginning it was really hard to recite them for me. Every time I tried to recite either of the sentences I would lisp, which brought about the therapist banging his ruler on the desk telling me to start over. "Say the words slowly, until you get it right. I would also practice at home after school while doing the dusting. Practice at home was worse, if I got it wrong there I would get a knitting needle thump on my head.

Dr. Seuss books were soon introduced into my learning regimen. I would take the books home from school, and have to sit right at Harriet's feet, and read them to her. One wrong word, and "Whap!" came the knitting needle. I tried to sit further from her, but she would not allow that.

So to avoid getting Harriet mad I did as she expected me to do. If I did not know a word I was to sound it out to her, she would then tell me the word, then I would repeat it to her, acknowledging that I understood her. I tried to make up one of the books I read by looking at the pictures. "And To Think That I Saw It On Mulberry Street" She actually got off the couch that day, coming at me, kicking me, and hitting me with her knitting needle.

I submitted to her putting my arms above my face not looking at her at all, telling her, "I WON'T DO IT AGAIN." She backed down, went back over to her knitting, saying, "You better NOT do it again. READ," she scolded. I started turning to the spot where she jumped off the couch, but she said, "No, from the beginning!" I never made that mistake again.

Part-way through summer vacation, Harriet informed us that we would be going to California to see her cousin Eva. Ted told us that along the way we would see the Grand Canyon, and the Mormon Tabernacle. If we were all well behaved we would also get to go to Knotts Berry Farm, and maybe Disney Land.

I could not help wondering if Eva was like Harriet. We took Interstate 80 all the way to Salt Lake City, Utah. Harriet wanted very much to see the Mormon Tabernacle. I have to say it was an amazing place. The Grand Canyon was next on our list of places to see. That was even more beautiful to see. I stayed away from the edge, because I was secretly afraid that Harriet would shove me over.

Each of our stops did not last more than a couple of hours, because we were expected at Harriet's cousins on a certain day. California was so fast paced. I had never seen anything like it. So many people, so many huge buildings, and so many cars. There were roads crossing over other roads, and Ted told us that we were not on the Interstate any more it was a Freeway.

Ted managed to find a motel near Harriet's cousins home. We unloaded our things at the motel, then headed to cousin Eva's house. Cousin Eva looked nothing like Harriet, she did act a lot like her though. Eva was tall, thin, blonde, and had a really dark tan. She was quite pretty. She was very snooty though. I got the impression that she had little need for children. It could have been that she just wasn't impressed with me.

Eva took us to her pool at the back of her home. Harriet asked her if it was ok for us to swim in her pool while they caught up with each other's lives. She told her it was fine. She asked me if I knew how to swim, and I told her I did. I did not know how to swim, however. We changed into our swim suits, then like an idiot I jumped in.

I didn't just jump in though, I jumped into the deep end of the pool. Eva had to jump in to rescue me.
I was never allowed at her home again. Ted told Harriet it was nothing to punish me over, he could teach me how to swim anytime. Harriet was so angry with me over being banned from her cousins home that when we went to Knott's Berry Farm, I was not allowed to ride on any of the rides. It also became my fault we could not go to Disney

Land.

I heard about that a lot of the way out of California. The Warrens did go back to see cousin Eva, but I stayed at grandma Warren's house when they went there again. Apparently Eva was just like Harriet in that aspect. The chlorine in her pool had ruined her outfit, which was an unforgivable act caused by me.

Once back home in Nebraska, things went back to normal. According to Harriet no one on her side of the family liked me. To prove her point I was told to read the letter her cousin had wrote to her telling her to never bring the ugly little girl she had adopted back to her house.

I spent my first summer with the Warren's avoiding her blows, keeping her house clean, and learning how to be the perfect student at school, of course the latter being after noon when the housework was finished.

That first year Ted never saw how his wife treated me, he was always gone. When he was home she was perfect Susie Homemaker, who put on that she loved me. When we were out in public things were the same, she was the perfect mother, who always dressed her children properly, never lost her temper, and always doted on how well they were all doing, especially me, since I was dubbed the problem child. Of course It was her love that was making me better.

September 22,1971, was my first birthday at the Warren's. I received a box of ugly green yarn and my first pair of knitting needles. That present meant I was in store for a new chore. Harriet was telling me I could make anything I wanted to out of it. "Yeah, right!" I thought to myself.

I thanked her, then asked to be excused, and started clearing plates from the table. I washed and dried the dishes, remembering my last birthday at the Wilson's. If only I could go back to see her. She would be surprised to see how self-sufficient I had become.

Harriet came into the kitchen after getting the little ones off to bed, I had all the dishes finished ready for her inspection. She inspected them, as she put them away. I was never allowed to leave the kitchen until the dishes passed her inspection. She then always said, "Good, now go take your bath, and go to bed." I always slipped into bed without waking Crystal, and I always fell asleep quickly, because I was always tired at the end of the day.

When Harriet was confident I knew how to get home from school, I started walking home. "That will make your legs stronger," she said. She always took Andy and me to school. One day she came to get Andy after school, but as I started to get into the car, she told me, "NO, you will walk." I shut the car door, and backed away. As she drove off, Andy stuck his tongue out at me.

I simply did not care, I just started walking home. When I got home, she was sitting on the couch knitting as usual. She looked up over the edge of the couch, and said, "After you put your things away, bring me the yarn you got for your birthday, as well as the needles."

I looked down to avoid looking at her, nodded, then went to put my things away. I came back out with the yarn and needles, and handed them to her. She took them, told me to watch her carefully, which I did. I had learned by then that she would only show me something one time, after that I would be in for a smack of some sort.

Harriet showed me in slow motion how to cast on. Then she said, "Sit over there facing me, and do what I just showed you." I learned what Harriet taught me quickly, I had no choice, there was no room for mistakes. Mistakes meant pain, and I was not used to the pain this lady so easily inflicted on me. Soon she told me to bring what I had done to her so she could see it.

I did as I was told. Harriet examined my work carefully, and said, "For your first time that is very good Anna." Then she slid it off the needle. She explained that each loop that I made over the needle became a stitch. She sent me back to my spot to cast on ten stitches. After every step of knitting that she showed me, I was expected to go back to my spot. I learned to knit in less than 30 minutes. I was doing it far from perfect, but Harriet was pleased with herself. I was just happy I was able to avoid her smacks.

It was Halloween, but I did not care. Andy and Crystal would be going out with Ted that night. I would be staying right where I was practicing my newest skill. Harriet always made a fuss over her other children, I was only openly praised if it was going to mean that Harriet would get the credit in some way.

When Ted came in from work, and noticed me sitting there awkwardly knitting, he asked Harriet, "When did you teach her that?" Harriet pleased with herself, said, "Oh, about 45 minutes ago." He then said, "Well I better get the little ones out trick-or-treating, so they are not up too late." I shivered at the thought of being alone with Harriet. I thought to myself, "I had better make sure I do everything right, while they are all gone."

When Ted went out the door carrying Crystal, with Andy at his heels, Harriet got up from her knitting spot. I looked down at my own knitting, secretly bracing myself for her blows. She didn't come to me though, she went to the console to put on a record. I was relieved. Her music seemed to calm her. I knew then that I would be ok, as long as the rest of the family was not gone too long. She went to get herself some tea. When she came back she surprised me with something she called a black cow. It was ice cream in a cup, with Pepsi poured over it.

I must have really pleased Harriet by learning to knit so quickly. She had a look at my little ten stitch project, took it off the needle, told me to unravel it, and showed me how to wind it into a ball around my hand. "Now do it again", she said. After everyone got back, it was bed time. I went to bed feeling pretty good that night.

Even though the Holidays were coming, I did not see them as anything special, because every day was the same for me with the exception of a new chore. Because this was my first Thanksgiving and Christmas with the Warrens however, Harriet's parents were coming to finally meet me.

They lived in Iowa. Andy was going to have to sleep on a cot in Harriet and Ted's room, the best linen would have to be washed and ironed for Andy's bed, because that is where Harriet's parents would be staying while they were visiting. I was going to have to learn a new chore. The ironing board was brought into Crystal and my room, and put up under the window on my side of the bed.

I learned to iron sections at a time, then I would take the freshly ironed sheets to Andy's room and make the bed. Ironing the sheets made them nice and crisp, which Harriet's mother liked. After I had that finished I was to look in the basement for the box that had Thanksgiving written on it, and bring it upstairs to Harriet.

With the house looking beautiful and festive, it was nearly time for Harriet's parent's arrival. When Andy excitedly proclaimed, "I think this is them," we all lined up near the door to welcome them.

Ted opened the door, Harriet's mother stepped into the room followed by Harriet's father.Harriet's mother was short, she had silver-gray hair that was twisted in the back and held with a beautiful flowered comb. She was wearing a very pretty flowered dress, with a wide belt at her waist. Harriet's father, was taller than his wife, he had white hair, tan pants, and a blue shirt with a tie.

Crystal and Andy were quick to go get their hugs. Harriet's mother put one arm around each child, giving them kisses and hugs. She gave her daughter, Harriet, a nice long hug. Harriet commented on how well her mother looked. Then she got to me.

Harriet's mother looked at me, wrapped both arms around me, and pulled me close to her.I smiled up at her. She said, "It is so nice to be finally meeting you Anna, I have heard so much about you already." I smiled at her replying, "It is nice to meet you too."

Ted went with Harriet's father to get their bags, while Harriet led her mother into the living room. It was time for the kids to make themselves scarce. Crystal and Andy ran off to play, I went off to knit on my bed.

I found out that if I stayed out of the way, and did my chores even though we had visitors there, I was safe from Harriet. I made it though my first holiday season, that left me feeling a bit more like a family member, because I was included more while Harriet's parents were there.

I received socks, shoes, more yarn, this time it was cream colored, and a Barbie doll with a case from Harriet's parents. Harriet took the Barbie and case after her parents left, "I didn't have time to be playing with dolls," she said. It was plain to see nothing would ever change. Harriet's niceness was just another of her put on acts. I wondered if it was hard for her to act like she liked me when other people were around, because it sure seemed natural for her.

The new year only meant that I was getting older, therefore I was able to handle more chores. Before I left for school every day, the dishes, vacuuming, and a quick dusting had to be done. I was always up right after Ted left for work. After school there was mopping the kitchen, and dining room, with ammonia water.

The bathroom cleaning was with bleach, with the mirror being done with vinegar water solution. Last was laundry, school work, then knitting. I got to where I didn't mind doing chores, as long as I was able to stay out of Harriet's way.

CHAPTER SIX
ADOPTION

July 17, 1972. This was a special day. Harriet, Ted, and I had to go to court to finalize my adoption. I thought I would be able to get away from Harriet until she explained to me what was going to happen in court. I was going to legally become a Warren, or should I choose, I could go back to the adoption agency.

I was ready to choose to go back to the adoption agency. Harriet must have either noticed the smile forming at the corners of my mouth, or she read my mind. She stopped my dreams of going back dead in their tracks. She informed me that should I choose not to become a member of their family, I would not be able to go back to the home I was in.

I would go to a state orphanage, where I would stay until I reached age 19. She insisted no one could love a problem child like me. If I chose to become a member of their family she would allow me to choose my own name. Harriet convinced me that this was my chance to start fresh, and cautioned me to choose wisely.

I despised this woman more than anything, but when it came to the Judge asking me if I wanted to stay with the Warrens, and with Harriet Warren sitting there looking at me, I folded my hands in front of me on the table looked at the Judge, smiled, and said "Yes sir, I would like to become a Warren."

The Judge looked to my new parents, asking them once again, "Are you sure you want to go through with this adoption?" (I was praying Harriet would change her mind just to hurt me). They both said they were sure. "Do you have a name picked out?" the Judge asked. Harriet said, "Yes we do! Anna picked it out herself."

The Judge looked at me, saying, "What have you picked out for a name, young lady." I replied, "Eva, sir." The Judge said, "So be it. From this day forward until the day you marry, you shall be known as Eva Warren! Congratulations to you all. Court dismissed!"

My heart sank! My chance to speak out slipped right past me. I was Harriet and Ted's legal daughter. Now I had to call Harriet mom. I wished I could have spoke to the Judge in private, but that was not allowed.

I had messed up my only chance of getting away from Harriet that day. There was nothing I could do about it now. Ted had driven his old white Dodge work van into town that morning, so he could go to work after court. He gave me a hug, told me to be a good girl for mom today, got in his old van, and backed out of his parking spot.

Harriet, who once again seemed pleased with herself, allowed me to sit in the front seat with her. I was rewarded with a new pair of saddle shoes from the mall on the way home.Once we got home, it was time to do the dishes that I had not had time to do because of court. I put my new shoes away in the closet in my room, then went to the kitchen to start the dishes. Harriet had already filled the sink with water - not a good sign that this day would go good.

I put my hands in the soapy water, then as fast as I had put them in, I pulled them back out. "OUCH!" I glared at her.

"The water is way too hot." As I reached up to put in some cold water, Harriet smacked me over the head with the cutting board sitting on the counter. The board broke over my head, which made Harriet furious at me.

Harriet dropped the silverware into the sink pushed my hands back into the hot water, then dropped a knife in the water, which sliced into the top of my hand deep enough to leave a scar. "Look what you made me do Eva." She tossed the cutting board into the trash. "You best not ever tell any one about this missy," she said.

That was it! That was all I could take! While she was at the trash can, I ran out the garage door, climbed through the fence behind the house, and ran as fast as I could up the hill. "Eva Warren, come back here, daddy will be so angry at you when he hears what you have done today.

" I thought to myself, "Let him be mad, I won't be there to hear about it." Over the hill I went. I had no clear plan, nowhere to go. I would just go until I could find someone to tell all of Harriet's secrets to.

If there is a God, he was with me that day. I had made my way towards town, but it was dark, and I was tired. I saw an open garage with a car inside, so I cautiously went in the garage, got in the back seat, and fell asleep.

When morning came, I was woken up by the woman who owned the car. She had come out to get in her car to go to work, instead she had stumbled across me. She woke me up, took me in her house, gave me hot chocolate, asked me who I was, looked at my hand, and listened to me speak about Harriet.

Soon Harriet's car was pulling up outside. "How could you betray me?" I thought. I was trapped inside this lady's house, the lady I found out was a social worker. She asked Harriet about the cut on my hand. Harriet explained it away saying that it was an accident, and if I had not run away she would have been able to doctor it up for me. Everything the social worker asked Harriet, she had an answer for. The social worker's hands were tied for the moment, she warned Harriet that she would be watching her.

That day only made Harriet sneakier. She was extra nice around people, but when it came to being alone with her things were going to get worse instead of better. She always made sure not to leave marks on me. When Harriet got me home, she made it clear she did not want to see me.

I got busy doing the chores I always did, desperately trying to stay out of her way. That afternoon Harriet decided she would teach me a lesson about defying her. She went to the basement, turned up the water heater temperature, waited until it had time to get the water good and hot, then went and ran my bath water. "Eva, come take your bath!"

I had no idea she had turned up the water heater that day. This was the first time she had played this game with me. I did wonder why she had stayed in the bathroom this time. She was up to something.

I found out the instant I put my foot in the bath water. As I tried to step out, she shoved me so that I fell into the straight hot water. The water stung my skin, burning it. I thrashed, and screamed, but she just kept trying to hold me in there. The steaming water hurt my hand, that she had cut the day before, so I tried to hold it out of the water, while fighting her to get out.

I managed to get out of the tub once, only to be picked up and dropped back in by her. Thank God, Ted had got off early that day. When he came into the house, he heard all the commotion from the bathroom. As he came in, Harriet was shoving my head under water. He pulled his wife off me, told her to get out, helped me out of the bathwater, wrapped a towel around me, then sent me to my room. I was sure she had every intention of drowning me that day.

Harriet got caught, but I must have done something that had provoked her into doing that. I told Ted I had just been doing my chores, when she called me to take my bath. I also told him that I thought she had turned up the temperature on the water heater, so he went to check it.

Ted went into the bedroom to ask Harriet why she had turned up the water heater, but she was too angry that she had been caught to speak to him. Of course, she didn't have an answer for him.

Harriet would never admit she wanted to kill me? Harriet packed her bags, and went to a motel. I had no idea what to do, I had caused all this. Harriet came back the next morning acting like nothing had happened. I steered clear of her, she stayed away from me. She would not even talk to me.

Cousin Eva invited the Warrens back to California for a visit. There was one condition, they could not bring me. I was happy when Ted told me I would be staying with grandma Warren.

Harriet took me to grandma's the night before they were to leave. Grandma listened to Harriet's orders for me, saying "Uh-huh," and, "of course," until Harriet said her good-byes. Once we heard the car leave, grandma said, "Well I thought she would never leave. Is your mother always like that?" I nodded yes, smiling, a bit embarrassed about how rude Harriet had been to Ted's mother.

"You will be with me for ten days, Eva, and here you will get to be the child you are. We just have to remember to make sure you have time to do those things your mother wanted you to do." Grandma Warren taught me how to garden while I was with her. We played go fish, and crazy 8s, both card games. We listened to the radio together, she told me stories about the old days, and always gave me an ice cream sandwich after supper.

Every morning while grandma was having her coffee, and listening to the news, I worked on the things Harriet wanted me to get done before she got back. I did not want grandma to get into trouble with Harriet. When Harriet and Ted came back to get me, Harriet seemed pleased that I had followed her instructions.

They thanked grandma for having me. Grandma whispered that she loved me in my ear, and told me to remember if Harriet found out I had fun there, she would never let me come back.

I was happy when school started up again. That meant I was away from Harriet. I was grateful for Harriet teaching me so much that first summer, I didn't feel so inferior to my class mates any more. I was sure that she must be plotting her next game for me though, and she was.

Harriet's next game was to give things to me, or allow me special moments, then when she could see I was enjoying myself, or I liked what she gave me, she would either take it away, or make me stop what I was enjoying, and it didn't stop there.

I was soon to learn for every good there had to be three negatives to follow.

For instance Harriet would pack my school lunch, and put a snack in it. She would make me a peanut butter and jelly sandwiches, making a heart shape with the jelly. She would also put cookies in my lunch box, and juice. After school she would make it a point to ask me how I liked my lunch. When I told her I liked it, especially the jelly heart shape, she stopped, making sure I knew that she had stopped because I was an undeserving, ugly little pig girl.

After that Harriet made me braunschweiger sandwiches, which I threw away in the trash can at school, until Andy got one of my discarded sandwiches out of the trash after school, and gave it to his mom.

Harriet took that sandwich home, and that day after I walked home, I was shocked to find the sandwich on the table waiting for me. I glared at Andy for getting it out of the trash. Harriet made me sit there and eat that sandwich, while she and Andy poked fun at me. "Don't be mad at Andy," Harriet said to me, "you are the one who always makes problems for yourself."

After Andy betrayed me over the sandwich, I decided to wait inside the school, until I knew he was gone, then I would start walking home, taking the sandwich out of the baggie it was in, and tossing it in the ditch for wild animals to find. Eventually that caught up to me as well. Andy got sneaky one day, and left school after me. He saw me toss the sandwich in the ditch.

I got home before Andy, I never suspected that he had tricked me. When he came in with the sandwich I knew I was in for it. Harriet made me eat the dirty sandwich. "When I tell you to eat your lunch you will learn to eat it, not toss it way," she told me.

I was grateful for the day that Harriet brought home a puppy for herself. He was a peek-a-pom, that she named Humphrey. He was so adorable, with a squished up face, and cute little snort sound.

The first time the poor little guy piddled in the house though, he was put on a chain next to the swing set. Harriet never went out to see him, she never petted him, she never fed him. Feeding Humphrey became my job. I loved doing that job, Humphrey and I had one thing in common, we both had made Harriet's bad books, so she could care less what happened to us.

Humphrey loved my braunschweiger sandwiches. I made sure he always got them. I would hide my sandwich before I went into the house, then later when I went out again to feed Humphrey, I would sneak around, and get him my sandwich.

The water faucet was near my hiding spot, so it was easy to pretend I was just getting Humphrey's water. I would set his water down, then sit on the bottom part of the wooden spool that Ted had brought home one day to use as an outside table. Humphrey would come sit on my lap. I then just acted like I was petting him, when I was actually feeding him my sandwich. I usually got yelled at for it, but she never caught on to my new getting-rid-of-the-sandwich trick.

On August 18th, 1972, Ted received bad news. Grandma Warren had suffered a severe stroke, and needed help being taken care of. Harriet volunteered, which meant she would be taking me with her to help take care of grandma. On the way to grandma's, Harriet made sure I understood that grandma was dying because she had taken care of me. I must have been too much of a handful for her.

When I saw grandma I couldn't hold my tears. She did not know either of us. I helped Harriet bathe her, and feed her. Harriet and I were there for two weeks taking care of grandma. I was sitting with her, holding her hand on September 1st when she died.

I was convinced from that moment on, that everything bad that happened to me or around me, happened in September. I figured that there was a higher power at work against me. If anyone tried to be nice to me, or help me, something bad would always happened to them.

September 22, 1972, my first birthday as Eva Warren was as usual nothing special, because I was nothing special. For me, my birthday meant Halloween was coming, then Thanksgiving, followed by Christmas. It meant soon the weather would be getting cold. I would have to shovel snow. Andy and Crystal had big jackets, with snow suits, to go play in the snow with. I had a wind breaker, and sweater.

I had lost all hope of everything. I was never allowed to play. My home life consisted of cleaning, reading, and knitting. School was totally different however, at school I was doing very well, with the exception of one issue.

At recess I would take my time going out so I could sneak food from the other kids' lunches. I did that because all Harriet gave me was the braunschweiger sandwiches, and I really did not like those. That was short-lived, when my classmates complained some of their food was missing, my teacher knew who it was taking the food. She pulled me to the side one day, and quietly told me to stop doing that or she would have to tell my mother. There was no way I wanted that, so I stopped.

The next recess I ran out just like everyone else. I was allowed to wear my new saddle shoes that day. The shoes had slick soles, that caused me to slip on the gravel. Face first I landed on the pavement, breaking one of my buck teeth.

I never spoke a word about it, because I did not want to get into trouble for that too. Shortly afterwards though Harriet called me to the basement. I had done the laundry wrong. As she was shoving me around she shoved my head into the iron pole between the laundry and the stairs breaking my other tooth. My two front teeth were no longer bucked. They were sore for some time though.

CHAPTER SEVEN
SEPTEMBER
STORM

I hated being a Warren. Every day I wished for something to happen that would take me away from those people. Nothing ever happened, no one could see how Harriet was. I merely existed, I did not matter, until September 22nd, 1973, when a huge storm rolled in.

I was knitting a panel of an afghan that Harriet wanted finished for her boutique, that would take place in November, sometime between Thanksgiving and Christmas. Ted had the younger kids with him, they would not make it home to celebrate my birthday, because there was a storm coming, so I was home alone with Harriet.

The lights flickered in the living room, then everything went dark. I had been listening to the storm, and had noticed the lightning. I wasn't afraid until a huge hail ball came crashing through the picture window, landing a few inches in front of me. As Harriet leapt off the couch, I just stood up ready for the darkness to take me.

I must have looked petrified, because Harriet came to me, put a hand on each shoulder, and calmly told me to go get as many blankets and towels as I could find. We had to sop up the water that was coming in. Outside the wind and hail was tearing the screens off the side windows, and there were shingles flying off the roof.

I just knew the darkness had finally caught up with me.
Harriet ran to the garage to get the board we used for camping, she needed to put it up where the window was.

When she came back I was crying uncontrollably. "Eva please come hold this up so I can nail it," she said. I did as I was told, my shoulders moving with my sobs. I looked at Harriet, and for the first time I saw concern on her face, and tears running down her cheeks. After we nailed the board on the window, she took my hand and we went to the basement.

There was a storage space on the north side of the house in the basement that was dug into the hill that we lived on. We sat in there waiting for the storm to stop.

For the first time ever Harriet showed me that she did actually care for me. She held me close to her, telling me everything would be ok, and how sorry she was that the storm had ruined my birthday. I asked her why she had saved me from the darkness.

I explained to her that the darkness had tried to come get me once before, but my dog Shadow had saved me. I told her I knew she didn't really want me, so she should have just let the darkness take me away. I made her cry.

Harriet chose her words carefully. As she ran her fingers through my hair, she told me it was not me, it was that she didn't know how to teach me and love me at the same time. That's when I found out Andy and Crystal were adopted as well. They were adopted as babies though.

With lightning flashing, thunder booming, and hail tearing at the house, I found myself feeling sorry for this lady I hated so much. Because I was adopted as an older child, Harriet was having problems because she was used to being able to bond with babies.

I reached up and wiped away a tear that was running down Harriet's cheek, then surprised her by saying, "It's ok mom, I still love you." Harriet and I bonded as much as we could that night, and I learned that no element would ever be able to take me away from the Warrens. I fell asleep with my head in Harriet's lap, for once I felt safe.

I woke up to Harriet gently shaking me. "The storm is over," she said, "let's go see what damage it caused." I climbed out of the cubby spot we had been in, and held my hand out to help Harriet down from where we were. I ran up the stairs to make sure Harriet was not going to be in any danger. Halfway up the stairs the lights came back on. I flipped the switch above the stairs on, showing Harriet the lights had come back on, which made her smile.

The living room looked like a tornado had gone through it. As we started picking things up, Harriet told me to go check on Humphrey, then go to the garage to get the shop-vac. I could use that to suck the water out of the carpet. She picked up the hail ball and put it in the freezer to show Ted whenever he would get home the next day.

Poor little Humphrey was drenched, but alive and happy to see me. I went and got the shop - vac from the garage, then headed to the living room to start sucking the water out of the carpet. After

I finished my task, Harriet told me to empty the shop-vac, and take it back to the garage, which I did.

When I went back to Harriet she told me it was very late, and I better just go to bed. That was the end of my 10th birthday. It was also the first time Harriet sent me off to bed with a hug and kiss, and it shocked me to hear her say, "I Love you, Eva." I laid there thinking about what Harriet had said that night. Was this another one of her tricks? Was this just a way to gain my trust? I fell asleep hoping for the best.

Ted returned home with my siblings around 9am the next morning. We all had exciting stories to tell each other. Harriet showed Ted the hail ball that was in the freezer. I kept our bonding a secret, because I did not believe that anything would ever change between Harriet and me.

I was right in my belief, with one exception. While Harriet and I were alone I almost felt like her daughter. When Harriet saw the need to discipline me however, she seemed much tougher. I merely tried to make sure I did nothing to upset her.

Harriet bought me a jacks set to teach me coordination. She convinced me that it would help me with the tension of my knitting. Harriet showed me one day on a strip of my knitting there were spots that were tighter or looser than others. Her explanation of that, was I had probably sat my project down to do chores, or have supper. When I started the project again my tension changed. It made sense to me, and playing jacks was fun.

Harriet also paid a woman who lived up the road from us to teach me etiquette. I went there for lessons only a couple of times. I learned how to hold a pinky finger out while drinking from a tea cup, and how to nibble instead of bite. There was a proper way to place a napkin in my lap, and a proper way to sit in a chair. Harriet's intentions for the classes was that some day knowing those things would land me a doctor, or a lawyer as a husband.

We were getting along pretty well. Then it happened. I had overheard her talking to her friend about a baby with a floating head. Being amazed at the thought of how a baby could have a floating head, I asked her friend about it when she phoned back. Harriet found out I had asked her friend such a personal question, and upset her horribly. My curious question literally came back to hit me in the head. I was dusting the kitchen table legs, when Harriet got the call.

I heard her say, "Oh really, I am so sorry," then, "don't worry, I will deal with this matter." When she hung up the phone I could tell her conversation had been about me. "Eva, come here," she commanded. It took me a second to be standing at attention in front of her. "Why did you ask Amy about her baby's floating head?" she asked. "You upset her very much!" I had not meant to upset her friend, I was only curious.

Harriet grabbed a handful of hair, and flung me to the floor. "I will teach you to listen in on others conversations!" She screamed. Crystal came into the room, having heard the commotion her mother was raising with me. Just as Harriet was getting ready to land another blow to my head, Crystal grabbed her hand, distracting her long enough for me to scoot away. I had not scooted far enough.

Harriet's final kick sent my head into the thick table leg. That incident left a nice dark bruise on the side of my face that I had to explain away by saying that I had lost my balance while dusting the table. I also had to apologize to Harriet's friend for upsetting her. It was after that I decided it was time to try to get away again.

Andy told Harriet that he thought I had been feeding Humphrey my sandwiches, so that lunch time Harriet decided to have Crystal and I eat our lunches on the front steps. Crystal asked me if my face hurt where it hit the table. I told her it did hurt a little, but I was going to get away that night. Harriet would never hurt me again, and they could go back to being the happy family they must have been before I came into their lives.

Crystal asked me where I would go, and what I would do. I was after all just a kid, I could not work. She asked me if she could go with me, but I told her I did not know what I would do to take care of myself, so I could not take care of her too. She told me she would keep my secret, which she did.

That night after my bath I gathered a few clothes, hid them under my pillow, and waited until I could hear Ted snoring. I snuck quietly out of bed, and made my way to the bedroom door. I got on my hands and knees, crawling carefully past all the bedroom doors. At the end of the hall I accidentally stepped on a creaky floorboard.

I froze! I stood there a few moments, making sure the creaking had not woke up anyone. I hurried through the dining area into the kitchen, then carefully I turned the door knob to the basement area. I opened the door enough to fit through, as I did not want the door to creak. I slowly closed the door behind me, holding the knob until it clicked.

I thought I had heard someone walking in the house, so I wasted no time getting into the garage, then out the back garage door. Oh no! I had forgot to figure Humphrey in my escape.

Humphrey, was always happy to see me. Surely he

was going to get me caught. I ran around the corner of the house, to the fence that divided the Warren's property from the hills. I pulled the fence apart enough to get through, and dashed up the shortest part of the hill. Once over the hill, I laid on my belly and peeked up to see if I had woken anyone up. Sure enough the back door light came on, and Ted was looking around.

I was too far away for Ted to see me in the dark. Not wanting to take any chances of getting caught, I scooted down the hill before I got up and ran. My heart was racing, my mind wondered which way to go. I knew I could not trust people to help me this time, based on the experience I had in my first attempt to get away.

I started following the first fence line I came to. I suppose I knew I would get caught eventually, but at that moment I was free, and maybe the next person who found me would not take me back to Harriet.

I felt terribly alone, and had no one I could turn to, because I knew that for everything I did Harriet could make something up. I sat on the side of a hill all alone, contemplating my next move as the morning sun began to come up. Because it was getting lighter out, I was able to see that there were cows everywhere. I was in someone's cow pasture!

Ted had told stories of a bull that used to come to the fence just after they had moved to their house. Being afraid of that bull, who was probably just a story to keep us away from the fence, I decided to get out of that pasture.

I could see a road not far from where I was sitting so I headed in that direction. Once on the road, I knew where I was. The road led to the lake. So I headed towards the lake, still not knowing what I would do when I made it there.

I must have walked miles that day! I ended up at the bait shop. They sold snacks there, so I used Ted's dollar coins to get some snacks. The cashier knew those coins were valuable, so he asked me where I got them. Of course I told him my dad gave them to me. That is how I got caught. After I left the shop, the cashier looked up Ted's phone number, and called him to alert him I had been there, and he offered to sell the coins back to Ted for the items I had purchased.

It did not take the Warrens long to find me. I was sitting at the lake oblivious of the fact that the cashier had ratted me out. Ted had not noticed me when he got out of his work van to go retrieve his coins from the cashier. I noticed the van, and saw him, but I was too afraid of him noticing me to move. I turned my back to the shop hoping when he came back out he would not see me. "Eva!" I heard him yell. "Don't run! Come to me now!" I reluctantly got up, and headed to him.

Ted put a stern hand on my shoulder and told me how worried Harriet was about me. I looked at him, and told him she was not worried about me. She hated me, and every time I did anything wrong she did something like this to me. I pointed at my bruised face.

Ted did not believe me, or he at least played it off that he did not believe me. He told me Harriet had said I fell into the table leg when I was dusting. I did not argue, I just got into the van.

Not another word was spoken as Ted took me home. Ted had a sad look on his face. I could not help wondering if he did believe me.

As Ted drove up the driveway he looked over at me, and told me to go straight to my room. I said, "Ok." With the van parked, I got out and headed to the door. Ted told me to wait, and go in with him. Harriet met us at the door.

"What do you have to say for yourself young lady?" she said. I stopped dead in my tracks, not wanting to say anything. Ted noticed my reaction, and pushed me past his wife. Ted told Harriet he had already got onto me about what I had done, and to leave it alone. I was sent to my room to work on my knitting. I could hear the Warrens talking, but could not hear what was being talked about. I imagined they were likely talking about me, and what to do with me.

School would be starting soon, and Harriet's first boutique was approaching fast. Harriet wanted me to get that afghan I was making finished. She enticed me with the promise that if I finished it in time for the boutique, I would get to go skiing with the family and actually be able to ski. I didn't believe her, but I finished it in time anyway.

The boutique was a sale of all the items that Harriet and her friend had worked on that entire year. I helped them set up for it, moving tables around, and setting up chairs for people to sit on if they needed to take a break. The proceeds from the sale would pay for both families to go on a ski trip in the Colorado mountains. I sat and watched people who came to the craft sale.

Harriet proudly told every person who looked at the afghan, that I had made it. The afghan was one of the first items to sell at $350.00. The buyer was an older lady, who had a soft voice. "My daughter made that." Harriet said. The lady looked at me. "I think I must have this," she said smiling at me. "You do lovely work!" she said as she handed the afghan to Harriet to hold for her while she shopped. I was pleased with myself, getting a compliment from such a nice woman.

When the woman finished shopping, and was paying she looked at me again, and told Harriet to make sure she gave me something nice out of that money to pay me for my lovely work. Harriet told her I would be going skiing. That sealed the deal. I was going to go on my first ski trip. I quietly told Harriet I didn't know how to ski. She said, "Daddy will teach you." Amy and Harriet sold almost everything at their boutique that year. It was official, both families would be able to do the trip to Colorado.

Ted found skis and boots for all of us. My skis were wooden, with black boots that buckled tightly up my ankle. When Ted told me to try the boots on and walk around I nearly fell flat on my face. The boots were very heavy, and did not allow me to walk normally. He asked me if they felt alright, not too tight, and they didn't squish my toes.

I showed him I could in fact walk okay in them, and they were not too tight, and didn't squish my toes. "Ok," he said, "you can take them off now." I did that, then went back to my chores. It was exciting thinking about going on this trip, but I was still not sure about Harriet.

CHAPTER EIGHT
COLORADO
VACATION

C hristmas came and went, then January, then February, I was beginning to think something had happened to make us not able to go on our family trip. Ted's birthday was fast approaching. Harriet announced at supper one night that we would all be taking a vacation to the mountains for Ted's birthday celebration.

It was the first day of March 1974, we would be leaving at 5 a.m. on the second of March.We had to load the car the night before. Harriet had made matching red coats for all of us, in hopes of being able to spot us coming down the mountain. Harriet didn't ski, she had problems with her feet, and was content to sit in the ski lounge.

Getting up at 4 something in the morning was not easy. I was glad we had loaded the car the night before. We only had to load pillows, and small items. Crystal propped her pillow against me, and went back to sleep after we took off out of our driveway. Once on Interstate 80 Ted and Harriet settled into soft chat.

I noticed every now and then Harriet would say, "Pa ditto!" then she would settle back into her chats with Ted. I would sit up a little to try to see what a pa ditto was, not seeing anything unusual, I would settle back down until her next pa ditto. Finally after one of her pa dittos Ted said, "Where? I don't see it," then he said, "Oh! there it is." A car with one working headlight popped out from behind a truck. From that day on a car with one working headlight was a pa ditto to me.

The drive to the mountains seemed like it was taking forever. We stopped for a bathroom break in Sterling, Colorado. After our bathroom break it was back into the car. Harriet handed us all a breakfast bar, "That is your breakfast kids," she said. After it was light enough to see well, Ted said, "Why don't we play the license plate game?" Andy asked, "What's that?"

Harriet explained the license plate game, and we all decided that would be fun. I had an advantage over Andy until he decided to start looking at cars behind us before I could see them beside us. Still it was a lot of fun, and distracted us from our boredom. The cabin we would be staying at was in Loveland, Colorado. It was literally built into the side of the mountain. The inside back wall was part of the mountain.

The cabin was a tall thin house with three floors. The first floor had a sitting room, a hall, stairs leading to upstairs rooms, a tiny kitchen, and a mule room. The mule room, (which was separated from the house by a door), Ted explained, was used by an old prospector to keep his mule out of bad weather.

The second floor had two bedrooms, a bathroom and stairs leading to the next floor. The third floor was just a bedroom. The kitchen did not have a refrigerator, it only had an old stove that Harriet was sure she did not want to use to cook meals on. Built into the side of the mountain right outside the back door of the cabin was an old sealed up mine shaft, that still had tracks leading into it.

When you are merely 10 years old that sort of thing is pretty spooky, especially at night. Because there was no fridge, we just set the ice chest outside the back door. It was certainly cold enough to keep our food cold, as a matter of fact, it was so cold we had ice milk in our cereal the next morning.

While exploring the cabin, Crystal and I ran across a snicker bar sitting on a table in the sitting room. Being kids we decided that it must have been left there for who ever wanted it. Crystal and I shared the snicker, not thinking any one else even knew it was there.

I should have known that all-knowing Harriet would have known about the snicker bar. I took the blame for the missing snicker bar when Harriet asked about it. The punishment for my greediness was that I would not be allowed to ski. Crystal told Ted that I had taken the full blame, but she had shared it with me. For that reason Ted talked Harriet into making my punishment less harsh. I would be able to ski in the mornings, but would have to spend after lunch with Harriet.

My first trip up the mountain was on a T-bar. A T-bar was a bar hooked up to the main cable, with curved sides attached to the bar. Some people I saw would hang onto the bar, letting it pull them up the mountain. Ted told me to lean against one side, and Andy the other. He said let the bar push you up the mountain.

That was such an exciting experience, until my jacket got hooked on the bar. I had to take my jacket off, which Ted retrieved for me. After the jacket situation was sorted, Ted showed me how to snow-plow. He told me that to begin with I should only use what he showed me.

Ted told me that was how to slow down if I did get to going too fast. Andy had ski-ed before, so he managed to keep up with Ted. I was not so good at this skiing thing though.By the time I made it about halfway though, I was doing pretty well.

I got a little too confident however towards the end. I lost control of myself. I plowed into the line waiting to go up the mountain, one of my skis went flying off over the cars in the parking lot, the other was with me. People in the line scurried every direction that they could to get out of my way. "AAAAAAA" (Crash) I ended up in a heap near the trash can.

I was embarrassed that I had not snow-plowed as Ted had showed me. Ted brought my ski back to me, made sure I was ok, and said, "Do you want to try again?" I said, "Yes, I can do it now." He said, "Try not to lose your skis again," chuckling.

Like they say, "Practice makes perfect." That is very true! By lunch time I was very good at keeping up with Ted and Andy. Most importantly, I didn't lose my skis again. With it being lunch time, I had to stick to Harriet's agreement to stay with her. I worked on my knitting, and watched people walk around in their boots. I wanted to go back up the mountain, but I did not let Harriet know I was having fun.

That night, after our sandwiches, we were sent to our sleeping bags. I was so tired that I fell asleep quickly. Morning seemed to come too fast, but I felt rested, and was ready to take on the mountain again. After our ice milk cereal, and breakfast clean up, it was time to head to the slopes.

We all situated Harriet in a cozy spot by a window, where Ted told her she would be able to see us as we came down the mountain. After her kisses and hugs we were out the door, heading for lines to go up the mountain. A few trips up the main slope convinced Ted that I was ready for the harder slopes. As I headed for the line to go back up the main slope, he stopped me. "I think you are ready for a harder slope, Eva," he smiled at me. I smiled back at him, and followed him and Andy to the harder slopes line. The harder slopes had bench chairs. Ted took me with him, because I had never been on one of those.

"When you feel the chair bump against you, sit down," Ted said. "Ok," I said. I did great! Ted even told me I had done it like a pro. We were so high in the air, the chairs went higher than the trees. I followed Ted down the mountain, only falling half a dozen times. Then, as I was waiting for the chair, I timed my sit wrong. I scrambled to get on before it got too high in the air.

I ended up holding onto Ted's leg all the way up

the mountain, where the person in the shed where the empty chairs went back down stopped the lift to help me off. Ted calmed me down, telling me it was ok, and that it could have happened to anyone. It didn't happen to me again though.

Ted was confident that Andy and I were good enough now to be on our own a little bit. So he told us to stay on that slope, and have fun. He was going to the hard slopes to ski as he liked. Andy and I did fine. We even decided to try the hard slope next to the slope we were on.

We went up the chair lift, got off ok, then noticed the moguls. I looked at Andy and said. "How are we supposed to get through that?" Andy said, "Well I suppose we go around each bump." Andy must have felt pretty confident at first. It was soon evident that he was frustrated. I carefully ski-ed to him, and told him in order to get back on the other slope we had to get down this one. I told him we should get over to the side so we would not be in the way of the good skiers.

Andy took my advice, and we made it to the bottom, vowing never to do that again. Three more times up and down the mountain, then it was lunch time, and time for me to spend the rest of the day with Harriet. We ski-ed at Loveland Basin for three days, then Ted decided he wanted to take us to Winter Park, it was supposed to have a great lounge for Harriet, and nice skiing conditions for

Ted.

Harriet liked Winter Park's lounge better. She could see us coming from halfway up the mountain. We finished up our ski vacation at Winter Park, too. I never wanted to leave there. A full week we had been skiing, and having fun, but it was time to go home. The next day we loaded the car, and headed out of the mountains.

I was sad to leave the most beautiful place ever. It was dark by the time we made it home. Ted told Harriet we should unload the car in the morning. She reluctantly agreed. I went to bed with the visions of our family trip still vivid in my mind. I hoped we would do that again every year, and was not looking forward to getting back to daily chores.

Since we were home from our ski trip, it was time to go back to school. One thing changed in my life after we came home. Ted started taking me with him on the weekends. He took me to do carpet laying jobs with him, and he took me to the family farm where his sister Mara lived. Mara was not quite right, Ted had told me. The family allowed her to live at the farm because she had nowhere else to go. Mara was the twin of Mark.

Grandma Warren was a Nebraska pioneer. Grandma had raised 14 children, several of them being twins. Ted taught me a great love for history, which helped me tremendously in my teen years.

One day Ted decided to tell me why he was bringing me along with him so much more. He said it was because Harriet and I did not seem to get along too well, and to avoid more problems between us, it was better for me to be with him.

Sometimes Andy and Crystal would come along, other times they had to stay with Harriet. Going with Ted made for a nice change. Ted loved teaching me things. I learned how to help him measure, stretch, paste, and cut carpet. I helped him load firewood at the farm. It was easy to talk to Ted.

Ted told me once that there was no such thing as a stupid question. He told me people learned by asking questions, so it was good to ask if I didn't know something. I never ran away after Ted took interest in me, and started taking me places. Not while we were living at that house anyway.

I still had to do my chores, do my knitting, and do my homework. The fifth grade was by far the best of my school years. During fifth grade we had to start learning how to do reports. Harriet was very good at teaching me how to help myself. We had encyclopedias, dictionaries, and thesauruses, as well as other great resource books.

Harriet was very proud of my scholastic abilities,

as she should have been, after all it was because of her that I did so well at school. Our teacher told us to do three reports on historic figures who we respected. We needed to include why we respected the people we chose to write about.

Since our assignment was history related I was very interested. I loved history, so I was excited to learn about my chosen historic figures.

I chose Abraham Lincoln, William Tell, Joan of Arc, and Helen Keller. I did my report on Helen Keller for extra credit. My extra hard work won me an award at the end of fifth grade. Of course, I won that award because of Harriet. She made sure to remind me that had it not been for her I would not have won an award at all.

Summer vacation started off with Ted bringing home house drawings. Ted had bought land outside the town near the farm. He got a great deal for the land, ($4,000 for 1 acre) and the only neighbor we would have would be the people who had sold him the land. As Ted and Harriet made plans about how our new house was going to be built, they decided that the rock for the upstairs and downstairs fireplace would be coming from the mountains.

That meant a trip to the mountains to a rockery, where they would pick out their rocks. Ted figured up how much rock he needed for both areas, then he borrowed a horse trailer, and flat trailer to go get it, that would save him on shipping. Our summer vacation ended up being that trip to the mountains, where, once there, Ted and Harriet decided to also purchase bricks for the house.

With both trailers loaded with rocks from the mountains we headed to the site of the new house. Ted had bought a new Dodge Van before our trip to get mountain rocks. The new van had made the trip great going to get the rocks, but the weight of the now loaded trailers behind the new van was making it struggle. Our trip out of the mountains seemed to take forever. Once out of the mountains however the new van did great, and Ted seemed happy that his purchase had been a good choice.

This was the first time we kids had seen where we would finish growing up. As we pulled into the entrance to the house site, Ted stopped, and turned in his seat, smiling. We all wondered what Ted was up to. He took Harriet's hands in his, happily stating that right there on her side of the van at the entrance would be a sign hand made by him, and he would use the tree that they had sat under when he had proposed to her.

We kids really did not understand the significance of that, but Harriet was almost crying about it. Ted carefully made his way up that hill, over the top of the hill to where we would help him unload all that rock, which took us quite a while. We found out that when school started back up, we would be starting school at this town, and there was only one school that all three of us would be going to.

When school did start back up, Ted drove us about 21 miles every morning to get us to school. Harriet would pick us up from school daily at 3:30, and we better not mess about after school. Our old house had not yet sold, but the Warrens did not want us to have to start school, then have to transfer later. They made the better choice of starting us where some of us would eventually graduate.

It was always easy for Andy and Crystal to make friends. It was not so easy for me. When I did make a friend, Andy was quick to make up lies about me to break the friendship. Andy told the first friend I made that our mom caught me eating from the garbage. That friendship ended with her passing it through the school that I was a garbage eater. Of course I had never been caught eating garbage, and I had not eaten garbage, but his lie had made my school life horrible for weeks. I became an outcast so he could become popular.

Eventually I was able to clear myself of Andy's lies, which began to make him out to be nothing but a liar. From this he learned to stop causing me grief, making him able to have his friends, while I was able to have mine. I made friends with the sher-iff's daughter, and two other girls. No one liked the sheriff's daughter, because they could never get by with anything while with her. I was not a trouble-maker, so I had no problem with her or her family.

One Friday Ted was going to be up at the new house doing some work there, so we kids would need to walk there after school. I found out then that my best friend lived on the same road that I would be walking home on when we could finally move into our new house. I waited for Andy to leave, and get far enough ahead of me so i could keep an eye on where he was. As I started going across the street my friend yelled out to me. I waited at the edge of the road for her to catch up.

We walked together until we got to her street, then she went her way, and I ran to almost catch up with Andy. I was surprised to see how much was done on our new house. The basement part of the house had the windows and doors already. The workers had the frame up for the rooms, and the outside. Even the staircase to the basement had been put in already. Ted happily showed Andy, Crystal, and I through our new house. We were each going to have our own bedroom. All three of us were happy about that.

CHAPTER NINE
THE HOUSE
ON THE HILL

O ur old house sold sometime in September of 1975, however our new house was not ready to move into yet. We had to box up, and move everything to storage. Ted rented two motel rooms, that were divided by a door, that we would have to live in until the new house was finished being built.

The main motel room was a kitchenette with a bed and bathroom. The other room was a normal motel room, with two beds, and a bathroom. We kids slept in the room with the two beds. Crystal and I shared a bed, and Andy had his own. Ted continued taking us to school, and Harriet kept picking us up from school.

Saturday, October 18th, 1975. It was still dark outside when there came a knock at the door of our motel room. Ted answered the door to a Sheriff. The Sheriff told Ted something horrific had happened in the town we were some day going to be moving to. He asked Ted to meet him up at our new house to search it in case the person who they were looking for had chosen to hide in there. We were all scared for Ted, but he told us it was his duty to go let the sheriff in to look around our new home.

Ted did not get back until around supper-time, and he had a grave story to tell us. A family had been brutally murdered, and there was a man-hunt going on. Ted showed us shell casings that had been found in the storage cellar at our new home. Someone had been there, but it had not been the person the Sheriff had been looking for.

The morning of October 19th, 1975, the person the sheriff had been looking for turned himself in, admitting that he had killed all those people.

My best friend was one of the family members who had died. The very same girl I walked home with, when we had been told to walk to the new house because Ted had been there working.

Harriet of course did not believe that I even knew

the little girl. She accused me of just looking for sympathy. My friend and I were not popular, we only had each other. We used to sit on the swings at recess talking. We ate our lunches together. She was my best friend. There was nothing Harriet could do about us being friends. However, she could, and did keep me away from the funeral, which was held at the school.

For many years I grieved for my best friend, never talking about it until I got much older. I have never forgotten her, or the few good times we had, and stories we shared. Stories of how we would grow up, and move away from the little town we lived in, to become successful women, with children of our own. We would show people we were somebodies, someday!

The new house was finally built and ready in time for Christmas. Ted had given the builders $40,000.00 telling them to build until they ran out of money. The builders finished all but the staining, and varnishing of the cupboards, and the painting of all the walls. Ted painted the walls with Andy, while Harriet and I stained and varnished the cabinet doors throughout the house. We moved in the day after Ted laid the carpet.

The Christmas tree went up right away. Harriet would only allow Andy and Crystal to help decorate the tree. Ted built a huge star to put on top of the house. Since this was a new house, Harriet had to show it off to her parents. They would come to visit for a week, and I would sleep with Crystal while they were visiting.

Our new house had blue shag carpet upstairs in the living room, dining room, and hall. It was my chore to rake the carpet with a leaf rake every weekend. There was a deck on the new house that had windows off the living room, dining room, kitchen, main bathroom, parent's bathroom, and parent's bedroom.

It was my chore to wash those inside and out every weekend as well. There were also windows downstairs to be washed, but not as many. I only had the downstairs family room windows to wash inside and out and Andy's bedroom window. My daily chores were to wash the dishes, then load them into the dishwasher. I know! It made no sense to me either. Also, I took out the trash, washed the floors, vacuumed, washed mirrors, cleaned toilets, cleaned tubs, and dug a hole in the garden area to dump garbage into.

While getting ready for Harriet's parents' visit, I had skimped on one of my chores. I had dusted the day before so I tried to skip on dusting the railings. Bad move on my part! Harriet, accustomed to grabbing my hair, did exactly that. She slammed my head into the twisted metal railings, she kept going until we got to the top of the stairs.

"Oh God," I thought, "she is going to push me down the stairs!" Harriet, still holding my hair pulled up, forcing me to stand. She turned me then shoved me. One step from the cement floor, was where I landed. Dazed from the fall, I tried to get away. Harriet was making her way towards me, I guess she wanted me to hit the cement floor.

"What she do this time?" Andy's question distracted Harriet enough for me to make a run for it. "Get her!" I heard Harriet tell Andy. Too late! I headed out the garage doors, then was gone.

I did not go far that time. I went behind the hill where there was a small cave, that I hid in until Ted came home. Harriet had no clue that I already told Ted what had happened, and how I responded. Ted told me to come in with him and go to my room, if he yelled for me I was to go straight to him.

I heard Ted tell Harriet that he had found me walking in town, and that he had picked me up to bring me home, figuring I had run off again. Then I heard Harriet tell him that she thought a good old-fashioned spanking with daddy's belt was called for. Ted yelled for me, I sheepishly came out of my room to stand in front of him.

Ted took off his belt. I, of course thought he was going to beat me with his belt. He grabbed my arm, and took me outside, shutting the door behind him. He told me to bend over his knee and cry really loud whenever I heard the belt snap. We were too close to the house for anyone to see us if they looked out the windows. I did precisely what Ted told me to do.

When Ted finished up our little show he stood me up grabbed my arm, and led me back into the house. Ted firmly told me to go to my room, and think about why I should not ever run away again. I hurried off to my room amazed that he had pulled that off, and grateful that he had not once let that belt hit me.

Since that Christmas was supposed to be a time for Harriet to show off to her parents, I would be reading "The Christmas Story" from the family Bible. That would show her mother how much Harriet had taught me over the years.

Moving into the new house on the hill should have meant better times. It did not though, everything spiraled out of control. After Harriet showed her mother how much she had accomplished since their last visit, and they had gone back to Iowa, things with Harriet and me slipped back to square one.

There were no neighbors to hear me scream, everyone was a friend of Harriet's, and once again I was a problem child that no one would ever believe. Since I had already tried my run away trick, Harriet tried something new with me. She made me wear my robe on the days we had no school.

My robe was two square pieces of cloth sewed together with arm holes, and neck hole. Harriet used the left over material from her robe to make my robe. The theory behind making me wear the robe, was since I was wearing just the robe, I would not be able to run away.

With the holidays over, and school restarting there were sign-ups for 7th grade cheer-leading, and track coming up. Harriet had me attempt at joining the cheer-leading squad.

The catch was that I would make my own sweater following the school's design. If I could do that I could join. Her plan was for me to make mine so nice that all the girls would want one. The trouble with her plan was that the parents had already paid for their girls outfits. Harriet's plan failed so my cheer-leading attempt also failed.

Harriet's next plan for me was to enter track, which I was very good at. Since I was good at track and was having fun, that was also ended in about two weeks tops. I was back to not being able to please Harriet, no matter what I did.

One morning just after school restarted, I was running late doing the morning chores. I did not feel very well. The heat from the sun coming in the kitchen window, combined with the heat from the hot dish water was making me feel light headed.

Harriet came into the kitchen, furious that I was not ready for school yet. There was a can-opener sitting on the counter waiting for me to wash it. She picked it up and smacked me over the back of the head with it, telling me to finish the dishes when I got home from school. I hurried to my room, got ready for school, then got out of the house as quickly as possible.

I was late to school, my head hurt, and I had not even noticed that my head was bleeding from Harriet's earlier hit. PE was my first class. The teacher looked over my head, and asked me what had happened. I told her I must have cut my head when I ran under a tree on my way to school. I very much doubt that she believed that story. My PE teacher sent me to the showers to wash the blood out of my hair.

After class the school counselor called me to the office to talk to him about my home life. I knew what I was supposed to do, and I did what Harriet had programmed me to do. If I made life hard for her, she would make my life three times harder. Remembering back now, I am able to see who was trying to help me, but at that age, it seemed I had nowhere to turn. That was exactly the way Harriet had planned it.

Harriet had to keep me convinced that I was the problem, and everyone knew it. One day the sheriff's wife called to invite me to come over for a play day with her daughter. To my surprise Harriet agreed to allow me to go play. She could not very easily turn down the wife of a sheriff, now could she?

Once inside the sheriff's house, I was asked a lot of questions about abuse. I was examined by the sheriff's wife, who explained to me that if I did not tell what was going on, and she could not find bruises on me, there would be nothing she could do to help me.

I really wanted the help, but I was convinced that there was nothing anyone could do. I told the sheriff's wife that I had tried before to tell on Harriet, but I was always on the losing side. Harriet received a surprise visit from a social worker because of my trip to the sheriff's house. That only provoked her. Harriet knew she could get by with almost anything.

Harriet grilled me, trying to get me to tell her what I had told them. I told her precisely what I had told the sheriff's wife, but she was not content with that. Harriet was certain I had said something to someone, to cause a social worker to come over 21 miles to check on me. I was never allowed to go anywhere after that. One day Ted came home with a dresser that he had picked up from the city dump. He proudly showed it to Harriet telling her that maybe one of the kids could use it in their rooms. Harriet had a new chore for me.

The dresser was an ugly green color, but that would soon change. Harriet bought Zip Strip to take the paint off the dresser. She globbed it all over the top of the dresser and told me to spread it around with my bare hands. That stuff was cold, and stung at my skin.

I was told to let it sit for a bit, then scrape off the old paint with the scraper Harriet had bought me to use. I worked on that dresser in the hot July sun every day, until it was stripped and completely sanded. My hands were sore from sun burn, and Zip Strip.

Too bad the social worker had not stopped by while I was doing that. Harriet had me paint the entire dresser black. It was then promised to me since my room colors were black, red, and white. I should have not done so well on that dresser, because after that the next chore was six chairs for the dining room table. Harriet had managed to keep me busy the whole summer.

First thing in the morning until noon was house-work, then work on stripping and sanding. After supper was laundry, and knitting. Harriet's newest form of torture was to have the family TV brought downstairs so everyone except me could watch it while I had to sit in the laundry room. The laundry room had no walls, so I could see the TV until she put a big chair in the way.

Harriet was a very sneaky woman, who controlled every aspect of her life to a T. To get Ted to move the TV downstairs she simply told him it was so horribly hot upstairs in the summer. Her explanation for the big chair being moved was that it looked better there.

To gain more control over me she started having me iron every single item of clothing that went through the washer and dryer. After I ironed an item, I had to take it to her, stand directly in front of her, and show her there were no wrinkles. If there were wrinkles, it was back to the iron to do it again. I was so happy to be able to go back to school in August.

One day, out of the blue, Harriet decided to start running my bath water again. I was 13, but she all of a sudden decided to punish me for the day she had moved out over the bath water being too hot.

That was her excuse, because I had acted so bad at seven, I would be punished then at age 13. Harriet's mind made no sense to me. One minute she was extra nice, the next she was trying to kill me. I have no idea how many times I wished she would just finish me off. She knocked me out cold one day. Had it not been for Crystal, Harriet would have had to explain my death.

I had got into her cinnamon rolls that she had made for Sunday breakfast. When she started coming after me for one of her hair pulling sessions, I tried to run. Her desperate attempt at shoving me caused me to lose my balance.

I hit my head on the wall as I fell. That is what knocked me out. She sat on top of me, closed both her hands around my neck, and pushed on my throat. I heard Crystal yell, "MOM! STOP! You're killing her!" as I felt myself slipping away. My last thought was, "Go ahead, finish me off, I'm ready for this." Harriet's slap brought me back. She was saying, "See, she's fine," as I sputtered, trying to catch my breath. Crystal told me later that night that my lips had turned completely blue.

I knew how to quietly take the screens off the windows of our new house, because I was the one who kept all the windows clean. I had decided to write Harriet a note this time. I wanted her to know why I was leaving again. "Dear Mom; I love you, but you do not love me. You pull my hair all the time. You beat me. You have everyone believing that I am your problem child. Mom you are the problem. I am afraid of you. This time don't try to find me. Love Eva."

I placed the note on my pillow. After I was sure everyone was sleeping, I took the screen off one side of my window and jumped up, then swung my feet out the window, and dropped to the ground. I stayed away from roads, making sure I kept to shadows. I followed the road that I took to school across town, then headed towards the highway.

Instead of staying on the road I walked along the fields. Once again I had no idea where to go or how to provide for myself. Without a plan I was sure to always fail. I would always be found and returned to Harriet. This time was no different. I was found, and returned. Harriet had folded my note and put it in her wallet, to use against me at some other point in my life. Once back home, I stopped running away for quite a while. Ted started making excuses to take me with him again. He even stopped laying carpet full time. Ted got a job at a local company, where I would go after school instead of home.

CHAPTER TEN CHRONIC RUNNER

Harriet had found out about a "Make It With Wool" contest from her friend. She decided that would be good for me. She bought me cream colored yarn, designed me a nice pattern, and set me to the task of making swatches to send my entry in. It took me 6 months to make the outfit.

I made a skirt, a sleeveless sweater, and a cardigan. I was very proud of myself. I won 2nd place at the state level, not good enough for Harriet, of course. She had expected more of me. She must have been a tad proud of me, because she bought me a charm bracelet to put the charms that I had won onto.

The charms were the only thing I received from the contest. A little sheep charm, tiny scissors charm, and knitting needle charms dangled from my bracelet to remind me that I had accomplished something good.

The pastor at our church told Harriet that church camp was coming up, and that might be just what I needed to bring me around. Two weeks away from Harriet was confusing for me. I was not allowed to interact with my peers past school hours. I was afraid to try to make a friend, what would be the use anyway? I spent much of my time in my appointed cabin reading. Harriet had given me $20 to spend on whatever I wanted.

I spent it on projects I made to give to her. I made Harriet an owl candle holder, praying hands, and an assortment of woodland creatures that I had seen while at the camp. The church camp had been at Chadron.

When camp was over the pastor took us to the church where our parents waited to pick us up. Harriet was happy to see Crystal, and Andy, but she chewed me out for spending my $20 on the "crap" I had made for her. The praying hands went into her china hutch, while the owl went into a cupboard. The little woodland creatures went into the top drawer of my dresser - she had no use for that garbage.

I am fairly sure those poor little creatures found their way to the trash eventually, I never saw them again.

My family were devout Church goers. Between age 14 and 15, I was confirmed in the Church. I attended twice a week classes. I studied the Bible, I accepted Jesus as my savior, I even memorized several passages in the Bible.

If you asked me to recite those passages now I doubt very much that I could. The one thing I learned from the Church that was in the town we lived, was that for all the preaching our pastor did, not a single person ever helped me. They all knew I was child in need, yet they all turned their backs on me, including the Pastor. Quite often their attempts at helping me only made matters worse for me.

I did get confirmed, earning me a beautiful white Bible that zipped up, and had gold lettering with my name on it. It was indeed another proud moment for me, however I cannot find it in my heart to believe in people who are so hypocritical. During my adulthood I only stepped into that church for my mother's funeral. I will only step into that church again at my father's funeral. After that, I will never return to that church, or that town!

I went to church every Sunday with the rest of my

family, the rest of the week I fought to survive. Do I believe in God? Yes, I do believe in God. I believe that God gave me the strength to survive my childhood. I believe that it was God who kept me safe from harm every time I ran away.

I believe that God has rewarded me with a wonderful, supportive husband, and beautiful, intelligent children, as well as grandchildren. I also believe God taught me how to forgive. When my children and I were stuck on the train tracks because my car ran out of gas. It was God that told me to look at the gas gauge, and while people passed me by in a hurry to get to where they were going, God helped me off those tracks safely. Guess God wasn't done with my children and I yet!

Summer break from school was filled with helping Ted, doing chores, going to the Warren farm on weekends, and swimming at the reservoir. We started going to the local swimming pool, but somehow Harriet got it in her head that the reservoir water was cleaner than the pool. My favorite thing to do during anytime was going to the Warren farm. My first time out there my aunt showed me the old homestead. A real sod house! I loved stories, and history intrigued me very much. How strong Grandma Warren must have been to raise so many children amazed me.

As Ted's brothers and sisters passed on, he purchased their parts of the farm. By doing this he ended up with 50% of the family farm that had originally been divided between 8 Warren children. He rented the land to local farmers to grow their crops. When farmers grew sweet corn we were able to fill our freezer with free sweet corn.

Harriet even made corn cob jelly out of the cobs. One year potatoes were planted out at the farm. After harvest, Ted took us kids out there with burlap bags to get potatoes. It was like a potato treasure hunt! Of course Harriet never went out to the farm. Dirty places was not her thing.

My aunt showed me how to collect eggs. I helped her feed the goats, pigs, and even the cows she had. The original house that grandma Warren raised her family in proudly stood out there for many years. I absolutely loved going there! I was allowed to spend the night out there with my aunt once.

Talk about spooky at night. There was a line of pine trees along the canal side of the farm. Those trees made it kind of scary after dark. My aunt telling me stories about wolves, and wild cats probably didn't help me much either. I tried to talk my aunt into keeping me out there with her, but she didn't think Harriet would approve of that.

The farm was where the Warren men used to go to get away from busy life to fish, and relax by the canal. The canal ran right next to the farm. Ted gave me my first driving lesson out there. Unfortunately it was the final time he did that, because I nearly backed up over him. I do not go out there any more, it makes me terribly sad to see it so run down.

Besides there is nobody who goes out there any more, because many of the original Warrens have passed on. At the writing of this book, Ted and his older sister are the last remaining children of grandma Warren.

When 7th grade started up, I was without friends at school. I was snickered at every time I walked into a classroom. I had study hall every morning, so I was able to do my homework. English and History were my best subjects. I did not attend any after school programs. Between school life being so stressful, and Harriet's abuse, I just could not cope.

Teens can be so cruel to each other. If one person does not fit in, that person is picked on by every single teen in the school. Especially if the school is a small school. I was old enough by the 9th grade to start doing odd jobs. My thought was because I could do odd jobs, I could also take care of myself. It was time to try my escape again.

After my last class of the day I stayed at the school. I knew Andy was too lazy to climb three flights of stairs in the old part of our school. So I hid up there in an open classroom, acting like I was doing school work if anyone came in. When the janitor came in and told me I would have to leave the room so he could clean it. I moved to another room.

I just happened to go to a window at the front of the school, right as Harriet pulled up. Andy got out of the car, just as I had expected he would. I turned off the light in the room I was hiding in, and pulled the shade on the window of the door, locking the door. I heard someone move the knob, but I think that was the janitor checking the rooms he had cleaned already. The Janitor always locked the doors after he cleaned the class rooms.

I went back to the window, and watched Andy go back to the car. Harriet backed out, and went in the direction of our house on the hill. I sat in that locked class room until I saw the hall lights go out. I knew the janitor had left that floor, because I could hear his footsteps as he went down the stairs.

It was after midnight, when the janitor left the building. I was still there. I went to the teacher's lounge, looking for food. There was a sandwich in the teacher's fridge, a donut, some chips, and a jar of coins. I took it all putting it in my backpack. I would need all that to survive. I did not plan on staying in the school. I searched every locker that did not have a lock on it, for anything that could possibly help me on the road. Then a brilliant plan popped into my head.

I would stay at the school all night, waiting for the right time to go home. Harriet always took the younger two to school at almost exactly the same time daily. Ted always left for work at exactly the same time every day. The house would be empty. There was at least one door that was always left unlocked, mainly because someone always forgot to lock it.

I would need more things to take care of myself. Money and food mostly. I snuck out of the school using the wedge by the door to keep it propped open so I could get back in after I scoured the town for needed items. I walked around town most the night, checking for unlocked doors.

The grocery store's back door was the only one I found unlocked. I went in, unzipped my back pack, and loaded it up with snacks of all kinds. Then I snuck back out the door, heading back to the school.

The wedge I had put in the door had been taken out while I was gone. I had to rethink my plan. I headed home making sure to keep to dark areas, and go down streets where I knew there were no dogs to bark. I went around the back side of the hill, in case anyone was looking for me. I went around the house comforting Humphrey so he wouldn't bark, and went into the garage.

The basement door was as usual unlocked. I didn't dare go to sleep, but I was so tired. I climbed into a big refrigerator box that was used to store our sleeping bags for camping. I curled up, telling myself to not sleep too soundly. Harriet's voice woke me with a start.

I heard Ted go into the kitchen, asking Harriet if I had come home in the night. I heard Harriet tell him, no. Ted told Harriet he would keep an eye out for me. Then I heard Ted go out the front door. I listened to Harriet's call to the school. Then she yelled for the two younger ones to hurry up so they would not be late for first class.

Once I knew they were all out the door, I climbed out of the box. I went upstairs, and got a bag out of my room. I put a few clothes, my charm bracelet, my knitted outfit, and my Bible into the bag. I went to Ted's sock drawer, got some money from his rolled up money sock. Then I slipped out the door, went under the fence, and headed across the hills as quick as I could, before Harriet got home. I was three hills away when I saw her car pull up.

I made it to Paxton, Nebraska, and stopped at the grocery store to get an already made sandwich. I left my suit case outside near a bench. When I came back out it was gone. I figured I just better count my losses and keep on walking.

Not far out of Paxton a Highway Patrol pulled over to ask me who I was, and where I was going. I told him that my name was Marie Wilson, and I was just going to the next town to visit my aunt. I didn't need a ride thank you. The Patrolman gave me a ride anyway - to the Police Station in Ogallala! I sat in an office waiting for my return to Harriet.

Instead I got placed into foster care there in Ogallala until they could figure out who I really was. I was enrolled into school in Ogallala, and joined after-school functions. I went to the roller-rink with my foster brother Mike. I did it all as Marie Wilson. For the rest of the school year I had a normal life. Except for the fact that I was not Marie Wilson.

Even back in the 70's police shared information. My information came across the Ogallala department's desk, and I was eventually taken back. I was not taken to Harriet though. They were not allowed to see me until my case had been investigated. I was put in a holding cell by myself at the jail. I was placed in jail as a chronic runaway. At court the Judge ordered me to have a 30 day evaluation at Geneva. Harriet and Ted were at court with me.

The Judge told me if I kept following the path I was

going down I would end up a criminal. I stood up at that point and told the Judge that I would never treat my children, when I had them, as Harriet had treated me. Well, he did not want to hear that. My parents loved me, and were there supporting me. I was taken from the courtroom by a Bailiff, and taken back to the jail. The next day at 9 am I going to be transported to Geneva for evaluation.

The first thing they did to me was make me strip down, for a search. I had to put on their clothes. Then I was taken to a room, to fill out forms. That was the evaluation, a book of forms filled with questions that did not pertain to me at all. It was an IQ test. So I wrote on every single page:

TALK TO MY MOTHER! SHE IS THE PROBLEM! I AM NOT THE PROBLEM! TALK TO MY MOTHER! They never said what they thought of my responses. At the end of my 30 days I was given back to Harriet.

She came to Geneva to pick me up, as a matter of fact. That was a not a happy ride home. Listening to her complain, it amused me when I told her I had heard her call the school. When I repeated what she said over the phone, her face just went blank. She stopped talking to me. The rest of the ride home was quiet. Harriet was starting to lose her control of me.

Harriet's next attempt of controlling me was to

smack me with a belt. I was getting too strong for her. She hit me with the belt one time only. As she went to swing the belt at me again, I let it wrap around my hand. I pulled it away from her. I respected Harriet too much to hit her. Andy was a different story though. When Harriet told him to get the belt from me, I smacked him in the face.

He backed up onto the fireplace ledge. As Harriet screamed at me, I screamed back at her. "Do you really expect me to just let you keep hitting me?" I asked her. "I am tired of you hitting me, and shoving me, I cannot stay in this rotten place you call a home." I went to my room, packed up clothes, and dared her to try to stop me again. Harriet backed off accusing me of being on drugs or something.

That time I got myself picked up in Sydney, Nebraska. I was put into foster care and school in Kimball, Nebraska under the name Jane Doe, because I refused to tell anyone my name, or anything about me. Once again I was found out, and taken back. A Judge sent me to a girls' home in Omaha, where I could not advance unless I worked with the people running the home.

I earned my way up easily. As soon as a girl makes it to level 2 you get to go on outings. My outing was permanent. I acted like I had to tie my shoe. I let the supervisors and other girls get far enough ahead to dodge off into the woods. While doing that I sliced my knee open on a barbed wire fence that was hidden in weeds. I cut my knee deep enough to leave a forever scar on my right knee. Those women and girls had no idea I was that fast.

I remembered from when I was brought into the girls home, that the Interstate was not far.I followed the river and the sun in a general westerly direction. Once I found the interstate I hitch-hiked a ride that took me almost all the way through the Colorado Rockies. The next ride I got took me to California. I was very lucky that my last ride was a VW van load of young hippies. They fed me, told me stories, gave me cigarettes, and sodas they could not have been much older than me. I made it to Escondido, California, where I met a young guy who allowed me to stay at his apartment with him. No strings attached, except I had to find a job, and help with the rent.

CHAPTER
ELEVEN
WORKING FOR
A LIVING

I was able to find a job, but it did not pay well. I made taco shells at a Hispanic taco shack. I cannot call it a restaurant, because it was literally a one room shack with a kitchen off the back. My earnings were not enough to help my friend pay his rent, so I ended up leaving, before he had to ask me to go. I traveled all over California, getting help along the way from complete strangers.

I was not too good at accepting rejection, and

my confidence level was very low. I constantly moved around, going to different shelters, but never staying long enough for anyone to be able to find out who I really was. I found people I could do chores for as well as a bit of babysitting. It wasn't much but I was surviving.

I learned that not all people could be trusted. There was a man, I never found out his name. He saw me walking by his home one early evening. He called out to me as I walked by. He asked me if I was hungry, to which I answered, "A little." When he asked me to come into his home, I begrudgingly went in. I remember telling him I could not stick around long, I had to get home. He got pretty rough with me once inside his home, but he did not rape me. Once again God was with me.

The man got a phone call, which made him leave. As he was walking out the door, he told me I had better be there when he got back or he would find me and kill me. He wasn't very smart apparently, because he locked me in his bathroom, which had a window that I opened and climbed out of. Obviously his idle threats were just that. I did not stay, he never found me and of course he did not kill me.

San Diego was where I ended up being talked into phoning home. "The world is not a nice place for such a young pretty girl." I wish I had a dollar for every time I heard that from someone. I was so fortunate, that I did not have a single person aside from that one man harm me. I am convinced that I had a powerful guardian angel.

I stumbled across a shelter for runaways in San Diego. It sat at the top of a hill. As I slowed my pace walking by, a young girl ran to catch me up. She said, "You're a runaway, ain't ya?" I ignored her. She kept up with me. She said, "Bet you're hungry!" I was starved, but I kept walking. That girl was relentless, and it was probably a good thing she was so relentless. I finally stopped walking, to listen to what she had to say.

That girl convinced me to go back up the hill to the shelter, but on the way there she told me about her friend who was dead. She was either a very good actress, or her friend had really died on the streets of San Diego. This girl's friend had been selling herself, and the wrong kind of man got a hold of her. She said they found her battered naked body in an alley not far from the shelter.

When we got to the old San Diego-style brick building we sat on the steps. I listened to her tell me how this place had helped her stay off the streets, go back to school, and most importantly this place had kept her safe. She asked me if I thought I wanted her help. Yes, I did want her help, but I did not want to go back to Harriet. I did stay at the shelter for a few weeks, and that girl did manage to talk me into calling home as well.

I had been out in California for almost a year. If I had to go back, I would only have a few months to live with Harriet before I reached 18. I spoke to Harriet, and Ted. They said they could arrange a way for me to come home if I could find my way to a bus station. I found the bus station, got on the bus, and watched California fade away behind the mountains.

The bus stopped at Sydney, Nebraska. I went to get off to get a soda, and a snack, but was stopped by a policeman. He had been told my bus number, and had been told to keep me on that bus. I asked him if he could at least take my money and get me something cold to drink and a bag of chips. He agreed to doing that as long as I stayed on that bus. Next stop was home.

As the Greyhound bus pulled off the interstate I saw Harriet. She was standing by the car waiting for me. I cannot say I was happy to see her. She met me right as I came off the bus. She almost had me convinced that she missed me. It is very difficult to forget the things that someone has done to you.

Harriet may have been able to put everything behind her, but I had not forgotten that it was because of her that I had left in the first place. She explained that I could come back to stay with them, but I had to get a job, and get my G.E.D. because it was too late for me to finish school where we lived. I agreed to her terms. Then she told me she had spoke to her friend at the local cafe and she had agreed to give me a job as a personal favor. I started work the next afternoon.

Harriet made sure she was gone when I started work the next morning. She was gone before I was ready. I walked to the local café introduced myself, and was handed an apron, a pen, and an order pad. The owner appointed me a section to wait tables in an area that would not get too busy for me. She needed to see how well I would do.

The café was not very large, most customers were from our village. I got accustomed to hearing "Oh Eva, when did you start working here?" and, "I thought you were in California." I smiled a fake smile a lot, and did my job. I worked there about two weeks
I always took the same route. Down our hill, across the road, right at the first street, follow that road right to the parking lot of the café. Enter through the back door, put on the fake smile, and get to work.

I was walking to work one afternoon, when I noticed a black pickup kept going by me. I deliberately tried to ignore it. After I got to work, put on my apron, and started waiting my tables, two men came in. The did not wait for someone to seat them, they came and sat in my section.

I acknowledged the two men, then went to get their water glasses. "Hi, miss!" one of the men said to me. I smiled politely and said "Hello." He continued, "My name is Mitch, this is my friend Tim." I said, "Nice to meet you two." I took their orders, all they wanted was a couple pieces of pie, and unlimited coffee.

Mitch asked me for my phone number, I told him my mother would not want me to give that out, and since I lived there I had to respect her wishes. "Well can I come back to give you a ride home after your shift?" Mitch asked. I agreed to that.

I finished my shift at 3pm. As I hung up my apron, and put my pen and tablet under the cash register, I saw that black pickup pull up out front of the ca Mitch got out, and came to the door. He smiled at me when he saw me. "Am I on time, or too early?" He asked. "You are on time, thank you," I replied.

Mitch had sandy brown hair, that was all wavy. His eyes were the lightest blue eyes I had ever seen, and one had a brown spot. The way he smiled at me made me feel embarrassed, and special at the same time. I went out the front door, telling my boss Abby I would see her tomorrow. Well, things don't always work out the way we plan.

Mitch opened my door for me, then started to drive me home. Then he said, "Would you want to go somewhere with me?" I said, "I don't know." I really felt comfortable with this man. He said, "What if I wanted to take you shopping at the mall?" I laughed at him. "Silly, the mall is 20 plus miles away." I informed him. "Would you object though?" he asked. I said, "No, I don't suppose I would."

I had a wonderful afternoon with Mitch, which turned into a magical night. I was too afraid to go back home after being gone so soon after Harriet and Ted had just got me back. I talked to Mitch about it. He told me he would take care of me. He did not want me to leave. He told me then that he wanted me to be the mother of his children. I was 16 years old at that time. Mitch was 27.

I loved the attention I received from Mitch. He treated me as though I was his world, introducing me to all his friends. I saw this as a way to finally get away from Harriet for good. When Mitch's job in construction took him to Texas I went with him. I called my adopted parents' home to let Harriet know I was ok, but I would never come back home aside from visits. I had found someone to love and care for me, and I would be ok. I did not call my adopted mother again until the birth of my first son.

Harriet tried to convince me that being with Mitch was not the life I should have. She pointed out to me that Mitch might be a drug abuser, and possibly an alcoholic. In my mind it was to late for Harriet to start caring about me. I was away from her, and I was ready to grow up whatever happened.

EPILOGUE

Child abuse is no secret. Big stories become news worthy, many cases go unreported every day all over the world. Some children don't survive abuse.

During my background searches I was told repeatedly that I was lucky to be alive. One woman was surprised I had survived to tell my story. She could not elaborate on that aside from telling me my files, that I will never be allowed to see, told her a story I don't remember.

From age seven to seventeen my life was struggle on top of struggle. I tried to tell people about my adopted mother. You know what the people I tried to tell did? They asked Harriet if she was abusing me. If you were abusing your child would you say, "Yes, I put this scar and that scar, and it was me who put that hairline fracture in her skull!" If you ask someone if they did something that is illegal, immoral, and down-right mean, they will not admit to it.

Harriet Warren was questioned on several occasions, and her answers were always the same. I was a problem child from day one. I had a vivid imagination. My scars were my proof, but Harriet explained those away by telling her interviewer that I was incredibly clumsy.

"The knife must have slipped into the water, cutting my hand. I must have knocked the iron over myself. I must have fallen and hit my own head on the corner of something." I never wanted to be there with them. Maybe I was running away to find my real mother. It was me causing her troubles, and she was doing the best she could to raise me.

Harriet Warren abused me daily. The abuse in this story is just a small fraction of what Harriet inflicted on me. My lungs are scarred from cleaning solutions being mixed, and her forcing me to stay where the fumes were. It made me clean faster to get out of the fumes.

Harriet knew what she was doing. Making sure if she left marks on me they were left where they could not be seen. My hair covered my head no marks showed there. On more than a few occasions a goose egg showed up there, but no one could see it. An equal amount of Harriets abuse was verbal. Telling me just how worthless I was, had a huge effect on me for a lot of years.

Telling me no one would ever want me, had an effect on me as well. The first man that came around that wanted me I latched onto for fear I was never going to get another chance. If you tell someone they are worthless long enough they begin to believe it.

For every mark Harriet put on me, I ran away. I ran away because I was a child. I did not know what else to do. My problem child record followed me until it could no longer follow me. I did not care at that point, I had made it away. Harriet could no longer hurt me, in the ways she had been accustomed to.

I was so confused for so many years. I loved my adopted mother Harriet. I hated her as well. I respected Harriet for everything she taught me. Without Harriet I could not have turned out as emotionally strong as I am today. Harriet started treating Crystal as she had me.

"I am sorry Crystal that you had to go through that. I should have stayed so you would never have been subjected to what she did me."

I had no idea that Crystal had taken my place until after Harriet's funeral. We had gone to the grocery store together, to pick up some items for my last family birthday dinner with my "family". On our way to the store Crystal shared her secret with me. She told me that for a long time she was really angry with me for leaving, because she had to take my spot.

That day was the saddest day of my life. After my dinner, and our remember this, remember that session over dessert, I went home. I would only see my sister again on her way to the Denver Airport. On Interstate 76 to be exact. She and Ted had saved a baby from under a rolled over car. I have not seen her again, but that is a secret I will have to take to my grave with me.

I learned everything the hard way. I chuckle now at parts of my life. Other parts I still cry like a baby over. I did finally learn the difference between my adopted siblings, and myself. Andy grew up to be an alcoholic, who has a public record of drunk driving, and domestic abuse. Crystal, I am not legally able to talk about, other than her made up name.

The rest of my story is in "Bring On The Rain." My second book will continues where "September's Child" left off. It shows how the first part of my life affected my entire life. What kind of relationships I had. What kinds of trouble I got into, and out of. How I raised my own children.

What rejections do to me. The list goes on, with the answers being in "Bring On The Rain."

ABOUT THE AUTHOR

"September's Child" is my debut book. I started writing it as a way to get rid of massive amounts of cluttered memories. Memories that affected me throughout my life. I have never been one to blame my present on my past. I believe after reading "September's Child" the reader will be able to see that a person does not always have to choose to allow his or her past to lay the brickwork for their future.

It is my belief that every person is in control of their existence after they reach adulthood. At which time they can choose to live in their past, or they can move on. Moving on means letting go. Letting go comes in stages.

Some can easily do this, others have to find their way. I had to find my own way, and it was indeed the rough way. I chose to have children of my own.

I chose to work hard. I took over a delivery job where I delivered vet supplies daily from Colorado to Nebraska. I taught myself computer repair, then taught others at the community college.

I moved to England to marry my totally awesome husband, Trevor. While in England, I became the sole owner of a Computer Repair business there. Doing my work in our conservatory, and with the help of my husband, I began going to people's houses.

I suppose I could have wallowed in my own grief, but I chose to move on in the best way I could. My biggest accomplishment was having my children, and breaking the cycle of emotional, and physical abuse.

My own personal message to my readers would be if you suspect abuse, either emotional, or physical, please don't choose to look the other way. I turned out being strong enough to survive. Not everyone is strong enough.

I do not believe in "bad children!" Instead of bad children, there is bad behavior. The bad behavior is learned from somewhere, or caused by something. If a person can get to the root of the behavior, they may be able to find the solution to the behavioral problem. The solution to behavioral problems do not always have to be fixed with prescription drugs! Granted there are some mental issues that is so, but not all behavior is a mental illness.

Amazon Reviews

If you enjoyed this book or received value
from it in any way, then I would like to ask
your for a favor. Won't you please leave
a review for this book on Amazon?
I read all reviews and they are greatly appreciated!

Click here, to leave a review on Amazon.

Printed in Great Britain
by Amazon